A Cultural History
of the
United States

■

Through the Decades

The 1930s

Petra Press

Lucent Books, Inc., San Diego, California

Library of Congress Cataloging-in-Publication Data

Press, Petra.
    The 1930s / by Petra Press.
        p.   cm.—(A cultural history of the United States through
the decades)
    Includes bibliographical references and index.
    Summary: Discusses the political, economic, and cultural life of
the United States in the troubled 1930s, focusing on the Depression,
the Dust Bowl phenomenon, formation of labor unions, the rise of
organized crime, and the Golden Age of radio.
    ISBN 1-56006-553-2 (alk. paper)
    1. United States—History—1933–1945—Juvenile literature.
2. United States—History—1919–1933—Juvenile literature.
3. United States—Social life and customs—1918–1945—
Juvenile literature. 4. Nineteen thirties—Juvenile literature.
[1. Nineteen thirties. 2. United States—History—1933–1945.
3. United States—History—1919–1933. 4. United States—Social
life and customs—1918–1945.] I. Title. II. Series.
E806.P76   1999
973.91—dc21   98-29895
                                               CIP
                                               AC

Printed in the U.S.A.

Contents

Franklin Delano Roosevelt would be elected to an unprecedented four terms as president of the United States. It would be his policies that would guide Americans out of the Great Depression.

The Failure of Optimism

When Herbert Hoover confidently took office in March 1929, the American economy was roaring along at a dizzying pace, creating a booming prosperity that showed no signs of slowing. Already inflated stock prices continued to spiral upward, igniting a growing frenzy of speculation. Neither he nor many other people in early 1929 realized that America's bubble was close to bursting.

The crash came on "Black Tuesday," October 29, 1929, when panic on Wall Street set off an orgy of selling and investors dumped 16,410,030 shares of stock. By the end of 1929 (two months after the initial crash) stockholders had lost $40 billion—more than the total U.S. expenditures on World War I. The stock market collapse in turn triggered a nationwide business depression that threw 7 million laborers out of work by the end of 1930. By the end of 1931, that figure had doubled again. To make matters worse, five thousand banks collapsed, wiping out the life savings of millions of people.

By 1932 the nation was sinking in gloom and misery. Hoover—a self-made millionaire with a reputation for integrity—might have seemed the perfect man for the job in 1928, but many considered his efforts to pull the country out of depression too little too late. He believed that to stimulate the economy the government should boost business rather than give handouts to the millions who were unemployed, homeless, and hungry. After Hoover's first term, most American voters were in an ugly mood, and it was the Democratic nominee who won their votes: New York governor Franklin Delano Roo-

sevelt, who based his campaign on the need for a "New Deal" for America's "forgotten man."

By the end of the business day on Thursday, October 24, 1929, the New York Stock Exchange had lost $4 billion. Thousands of investors—many of them ordinary working people—were financially ruined.

Over his next two terms in office, FDR's decisive legislation would be just that—a New Deal for America's forgotten working men and women. His New Deal programs were sparked by the three R's: relief, recovery, and reform. Government relief agencies were set up to make sure the unemployed could feed their children and save their homes from foreclosure. Recovery programs created government works projects to provide people with jobs, and reform legislation reorganized banks and the stock market, guaranteed workers the right to unionize, and regulated unsafe working conditions in many major industries. Some programs worked, some didn't, but the overall effect of FDR's

New Deal was to slowly pull the country out of its terrible economic and psychological depression.

The real story of the 1930s is how individual families endured and survived, whether battling the despair of hunger and unemployment in the city or the fear of unending drought and forced migration in the dust bowl of the Great Plains. It is the story of people fighting for the right to earn a decent wage in safe working conditions. But it is also the story of how people coped and had fun, of the news events that shaped their daily lives, and of how radio, music, movies, and sports kept their hopes alive and offered them an escape from the dreary day-to-day chore of making do and staying alive.

Chapter One

For the millions of unemployed people in cities like New York, the Great Depression was a brutal time of breadlines and tent cities, of starvation and suicides so routine that they often went unreported.

"Brother, Can You Spare a Dime?"

Herbert Hoover's term in office began well enough. It was the last year of the twenties—the decade of profits, big business, and optimism. When Hoover, a Republican, was sworn in on March 4, 1929, the country's gross national product (GNP) was at an all-time high of $204 billion and on Wall Street, the stock market was soaring. In his inaugural address,

Hoover voiced great optimism, describing a thriving nation that was expanding its social and economic systems. He pledged increased support for education, public health, and law enforcement in the nation's growing cities.

The majority of the voting public initially saw Hoover as a model of hard work, efficiency, and dedication. He had both their trust and support—

that is, until the bottom fell out of the stock market in October 1929. Then public opinion quickly changed.

Before long, Herbert Hoover's name was being linked to the hardships of depression life: the shantytowns that sprang up on the outskirts of major cities became "Hoovervilles" and the newspapers the homeless used to stay warm became known as "Hoover blankets." People with empty pants pockets turned inside-out were said to be waving "Hoover flags." Even today, for many people the name Hoover still conjures up images of breadlines, soup kitchens, and Wall Street suicides.

That is an unfair misperception. Hoover was more a scapegoat for the Great Depression than its cause. He was neither incompetent nor the insensitive defender of the wealthy the Democrats were quick to make him out to be.

Hoover, a Man Unfairly Remembered

Herbert Clark Hoover, the thirty-first president, was a Quaker, an engineer, and a nonpolitician from California who had never before run for public office. He was also one of the self-made millionaires of the prosperous twenties.

Above all, Hoover had tremendous faith in the American traditions of indi-

As the man at the top when the bottom fell out of the American economy, Herbert Hoover's name still conjures up images of breadlines and homeless people, but he was more a victim of bad timing than incompetence and insensitivity.

vidual freedom and free enterprise. Orphaned as a young boy, it was his own hard work, ability, and initiative that had made him a millionaire and this same system of capitalism, he firmly believed, was strong enough to withstand the stock market crash and to revive the American economy on its own. In his eyes, to give the federal government the power to regulate free enterprise was to threaten the very foundations the country had been built upon.

Even more unthinkable in his eyes was a system that empowered the government to give cash directly to the homeless and unemployed. Hoover believed that such a system would undermine the initiative, self-respect, and individual freedom of millions of Americans, not to mention bankrupt the federal government and lead to massive corruption and waste. "If you let the federal government help the individual," he said, "soon the federal government will control that individual."[1]

Instead of advocating government intervention, Hoover encouraged business leaders to take the initiative to strengthen the economy and get industry moving again. He believed bolstering industry would benefit everyone because it would create jobs and the increased profits would "trickle down" and stimulate the economy on every level. He stressed it was not the role of government to help the homeless and unemployed, that private community charity organizations could and should do that most effectively. Above all, he felt, it was crucial to keep an optimistic attitude. Prosperity, he assured everyone, was just around the corner.

Hoover's Plan of Action

When it became obvious that business leaders were failing to rouse

the economy on their own, President Hoover did finally supply a degree of federal relief to beleaguered farmers

The Bonus Army

One of the events that helped turn public sentiment against President Hoover occurred in June 1932, when over twenty thousand unemployed World War I veterans with hungry families marched to Washington to demand the war bonuses that Congress had promised them. Congress had voted to pay them in 1945, but the impoverished ex-soldiers were desperately in need of the money and asked Congress to pass a new bill making the money available at once. While they waited, the men took shelter in empty federal buildings, put up tents, or built packing-crate shacks on mud flats not far from the Capitol.

Congress heard their request but turned it down, although they did later vote to at least pay the men's passage home. Discouraged, about five thousand of the veterans left, but most of them stayed in protest.

By July, President Hoover decided to have local police evacuate the veterans living in the unused federal buildings. Two veterans died in the resulting skirmish, prompting Hoover to call in federal troops under the command of General Douglas MacArthur. The troops used drawn sabers, fixed bayonets, and tear gas to force men out of the federal buildings, then marched on the mud flats, tossing tear gas bombs into the settlement and then setting the tents and shacks on fire with torches, injuring one thousand of the veterans in the process.

FDR's supporters tried to make Hoover a non-person, ordering that his name be removed from projects such as the Hoover Dam. FDR's secretary of the interior, Harold Ickes, re-named it the Boulder Dam, which remained its official name until President Truman changed it back in the late 1940s.

tion Finance Corporation. Set up in early 1932, the RFC was empowered to lend up to $2 billion to banks, railroads, building and loan associations, and insurance companies. He also asked Congress to appropriate money for public works such as the Hoover Dam project to create more jobs and help energize the building industry. To aid farmers, Hoover urged the Federal Farm Board to buy up large quantities of surplus crops in the hope that this would stop farm income from spiraling further downward. Yet at the same time, he remained adamantly opposed to any kind of government relief payments to the unemployed.

For the most part, even these substantial relief efforts in the last year of his presidency failed to improve Hoover's popularity with voters. By late 1932 the country was angry. Unemployed masses, evicted for nonpayment of rent and without food for their children, threatened to loot grocery stores unless they were given food. In 1932 alone, 273,000 homeowners lost

and financial institutions. He proposed that Congress establish the Reconstruc-

their homes to foreclosure; by early 1933, they were losing them at a rate of a thousand a day. For a while, 5,000 homeless people sold apples on the streets of New York City.

Many of these disgruntled and bitter Americans blamed Hoover personally for the country's terrible depression, calling it the "Hoover depression." Author Russell Baker writes that when he was a young boy his Aunt Pat had

By 1933 thousands of desperate unemployed men and women in American cities were reduced to selling apples on street corners.

told him, "People were starving because of Herbert Hoover. My mother was out of work because of Herbert Hoover, and their fatherless children were being packed away to orphanages . . . by Herbert Hoover."[2]

A Promise of a New Deal

After three years of devastating depression, the Republicans, for better or worse, loyally renominated Hoover for the presidency, while the Democrats picked Franklin Delano Roosevelt, the popular and successful governor of New York as their candidate. As soon as he heard that he had been picked as the nominee, FDR flew to the convention in Chicago and broke tradition by accepting the nomination in person. (It was customary to wait a few weeks.)

In his acceptance speech to the throng of cheering delegates, Roosevelt declared, "Let it be the task from now on for our party to break foolish traditions."[3] He ended his rousing speech by saying, "I pledge you, I pledge myself, to a New Deal for the American People."[4] Those two words—New Deal—would become the trademark of both his campaign and the decade.

On election day it became clear that voters blamed the party in power for the depression. In an overwhelming landslide, Roosevelt's activist approach and personal charm enabled him to

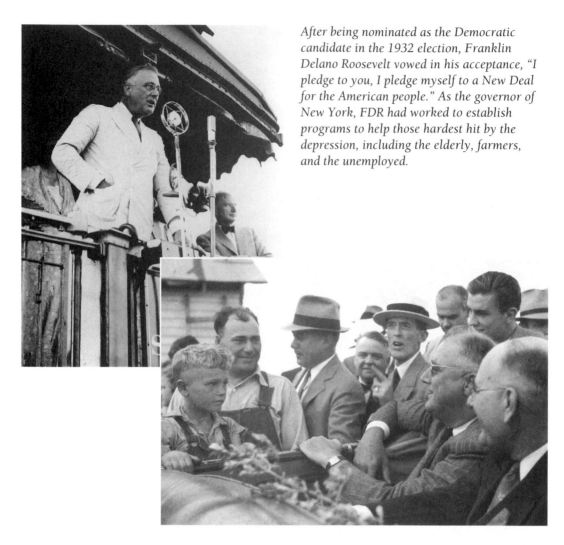

After being nominated as the Democratic candidate in the 1932 election, Franklin Delano Roosevelt vowed in his acceptance, "I pledge to you, I pledge myself to a New Deal for the American people." As the governor of New York, FDR had worked to establish programs to help those hardest hit by the depression, including the elderly, farmers, and the unemployed.

carry forty-two of the forty-eight states. The Democrats also won a large majority in Congress.

Nothing to Fear but Fear Itself

In his inaugural address on March 4, 1933, President Roosevelt assured the American people that their great nation would endure as it had endured in the past, that it would revive and that it would prosper. Perhaps his most famous words were uttered in that speech: "Let me assert my firm belief that the only thing we have to fear is fear itself—nameless, unreasoning, unjustified terror which paralyzes needed efforts to convert retreat into advance."[5]

Describing the nationwide poverty and despair, he stated that "only a foolish optimist can deny the dark realities of the moment." He repeatedly stressed the need for immediate action, for treating the depression as if it had the emergency and immediacy of a war. He went on to warn that in these desperate times, "It may be that an unprecedented demand and need for undelayed action may call for temporary departure from that normal balance of public proce-dure."[6] Roosevelt was laying the groundwork to potentially override Congress, knowing that if he was able to secure public support first, Congress would have to cooperate with him.

The First Hundred Days

The depression worsened in the months preceding Roosevelt's inauguration. One out of every three wage and salary earners—12.5 million men and women—were out of a job. Those

Overwhelming economic pressures faced President-elect Roosevelt as he took the oath of office from Chief Justice Charles Evans Hughes. Yet his inaugural address to the nation was optimistic, assuring the American people that their country would not only endure, but revive and prosper. "The only thing we have to fear," he said, "is fear itself."

who had jobs often fared little better with salaries of only four to ten cents an hour. Many American children had not had milk in months; in New York it was estimated that at least a fifth of the children in public schools were suffering from serious malnutrition. Many people feared that conditions would soon make people so desperate that a bloody revolution would break out.

Roosevelt's most urgent problem during his first one hundred days in office, however, was the impending collapse of the banking system. Since the start of the depression, more than four thousand banks had failed. In the last months of 1932, Nevada, Michigan, and Louisiana were all forced to suspend bank activities. On the morning of inauguration day in March 1933, the richest state in the Union, New York, followed suit. It was only a matter of days until the U.S. banking system would collapse entirely. In the last two weeks of Hoover's presidency, depositors all over the country had made a desperate run on the banks, withdrawing and hoarding more than $1 billion in cash.

On his first full day in office, FDR called Congress to convene a special session to draft an emergency banking bill. The next day he issued a proclamation declaring a national holiday during which all banks would be temporarily closed.

On March 9, Congress passed the Emergency Banking Act, which left it to the Treasury Department to decide which banks would be allowed to reopen and under what conditions. Eventually, over half the banks were allowed to reopen, with their deposits now ensured by the federal government. The Federal Deposit Insurance Corporation (FDIC) granted government insurance for bank deposits in

Many of the nation's banks, such as this one in Haverill, Iowa, had speculated heavily with their depositors' money and were wiped out by the falling prices.

It's Up to the Women

Although women increased their political activism during their emancipation efforts in the twenties, it was not until the early New Deal years that they were appointed to many government positions for the first time. One of the most remarkable and politically persuasive women of the thirties was the First Lady herself, Eleanor Roosevelt.

In the course of getting settled in at the White House in 1933, Eleanor published her first book, a compilation of essays called *It's Up to the Women*. In it, she covered a wide spectrum of women's issues, from advice on such topics as household budgets and child rearing to fervent appeals to women to lead in the movement for social justice. The book was a call to action. Eleanor's primary concerns were peace, the abolition of poverty, a concern for youth, women's rights, and the rights of minorities in general. She urged women to support trade unions, to set up consumer groups, and to participate in politics. The book, however, was just a beginning. Eleanor was soon dictating as many as one hundred letters a day, speaking to countless women's groups, and volunteering her time to soup kitchens and other charitable organizations.

Another way in which Eleanor Roosevelt provided women with a forum for their views and concerns was the press conference, in which she often focused on how the New Deal programs affected women and minorities. The First Lady also wrote two columns for the monthly magazine *Democratic Digest* published by the Women's Division of the Democratic National Committee. One called "Ask Mrs. Roosevelt" gave information about women's activities in politics and government, and the other, "My Day," gave Mrs. Roosevelt's personal impressions of how the depression was affecting the country.

member banks of the Federal Reserve system. In the first three weeks after banks opened again, customers' confidence returned and people began redepositing their money.

FDR worked with a special session of Congress during the first one hundred days of his presidency. Together, they passed legislation of unprecedented scope to stimulate industrial recovery, assist hardship victims, restore jobs, and guarantee minimum living standards. They set up special agencies to support farm prices, assist business and labor, insure bank deposits, regulate the stock market, subsidize home and farm mortgage payments, and aid the unemployed.

Over time, these measures began to revive people's confidence in the economy. Direct relief saved millions of unemployed people and their families from starvation, while reform laws affecting business, monetary and stock market regulations were passed to prevent future economic crises.

Reform Measures

The Emergency Banking Act, though it prevented a collapse of the U.S. banking system, did not do much to bolster the faith that America's European trading partners had in the U.S. dollar.

At the time, American currency was backed by gold, as were the currencies of France, Germany, and other countries in Europe. An ounce of gold was worth a certain number of German marks, for example, or American dollars. (The United States actually stored that gold in Fort Knox, Kentucky.) As America's economic crisis deepened, more and more foreign investors began to demand payment directly in gold instead of paper dollars, then pulled out of American markets altogether, taking the gold out of the country with them. The gold supply in the United States was being depleted so rapidly that if something were not done soon, the U.S. dollar would become worthless.

On April 19, FDR took U.S. currency off the gold standard, but not without explaining his reasons directly to the people in one of his radio fireside chats. Instead of panic, most people felt relief that the monetary crisis was out in the open and that someone was at least trying to do something about it.

Another issue early New Deal reform laws addressed was prohibition. Although there was already debate in Congress about when and how to end the decade-long ban on the sale, manufacture, and consumption of alcohol in the United States, FDR felt it would bolster public spirits if at least part of the prohibition on alcohol could be lifted immediately. In early March he urged Congress to pass an amendment to the Volstead Act to allow the brewing of low-alcohol-content 3.2 beer; on April 7 beer was sold and consumed legally in the United States for the first time since 1920.

Images of the Depression

All-too familiar images came to represent city life in the early thirties: breadlines and soup kitchens, former stock brokers and corporate executives reduced to selling apples out of crates on street corners, and the beaten and shamed expressions of evicted families huddled on the sidewalk with their few meager possessions. It was unusual to walk down the street without seeing men carrying signs reading I WILL WORK FOR FOOD.

As journalist W. J. Cash wrote: "Everybody was either ruined beyond his wildest previous fears or stood in peril of such ruin. And the general psychological reaction? . . . bewilderment and terror."[7] Even four years later, after President Roosevelt's New Deal policies had been put into effect,

FDR said in his second inauguration speech, "I see one-third of a nation ill-housed, ill-clad, ill-nourished."[8]

Not everyone was unemployed or homeless, of course, but the economy was so devastated that even those with jobs and a roof over their heads struggled to make ends meet.

Unemployment Reaches an All-Time High

Between 1929 and 1933 alone, over eighty-five thousand businesses failed. Construction of new houses, office buildings, and factories virtually stopped. No official figures were kept, but historians estimate that by 1933 about one-fourth of the country's labor force—between 12 and 15 million people—was unemployed.

Millions of others could find only occasional or part-time work, often earning less than enough to feed their families. Even those who managed to keep their regular, full-time jobs often had their paychecks cut so severely that they could barely pay their bills. To make matters worse, more than 9 million savings accounts had been wiped out in the banking crisis.

Many men felt demoralized after months and even years of looking for work. Humiliated at their inability to support their families, they spent their days in parks and other public places. Some left their families to become hobos; others were reduced to stealing to feed their children.

Competition for jobs was desperate and discouraging. A drifter named Ed Paulson who left his family to ride the rails as a hobo described in Studs Terkel's oral history *Hard Times* how thousands of men would show up on a mere rumor that someone was going to start a construction project:

So the next morning you get up at five o'clock and you dash over there. You got a big tip. There's three thousand men there, carpenters, cement men, guys who knew machinery and everything else. . . . These were fathers, eighty percent of them. More and more men were after fewer and fewer jobs. . . . They just wanted to go to work and they just couldn't understand.[9]

Songwriter Yip Harburg recalled how he came to write the lyrics for a '30s hit tune:

The prevailing greeting at that time on every block you passed, by some poor guy coming up was: "Can you spare a dime?" or "Can you spare something for a cup of coffee?" . . . I thought, "Brother, can you spare a dime?" could be a beautiful title. If I could only work it out by telling people, through the song, it isn't just a man asking for a dime. This is a man who says: I built the railroads. I built that tower. I fought your wars. . . . Why

the hell should I be standing in line now? What happened to all this wealth I created?[10]

It was not unusual to find engineers and architects working as gas station attendants or to see college graduates with Ph.D.s working as office aides or running elevators in department stores. Not only industries and construction sites but banks, insurance agencies, shops, and offices of every kind had shut down. Businesses that remained open laid off a good part of their workforce and drastically cut wages.

Every morning hundreds of desperate, unemployed men showed up at hiring halls, docks, or public employment offices pushing and fighting to be among the lucky five or six that might get hired for a day's work. Often, the unlucky ones didn't return home, but instead sat glumly in parks or poolrooms all day or nursed nickel cups of coffee at a neighborhood diner. Some spent their days at the public library to avoid the humiliation of going back home empty-handed.

After months, often years, of futile daily job hunts, many men simply stopped looking. Some left their families and became vagrants. In an October 7, 1932, article, the *New York Times* reported:

Fifty-four men were arrested yesterday morning for sleeping or idling in the arcade connecting with the subway through 45 West Forty-second Street, but most of them considered their unexpected meeting with a raiding party of ten policemen as a stroke of luck because it brought them free meals yesterday and shelter last night from the sudden change in weather.[11]

During the 1930s, a woman's chances for employment were often even slimmer. "Getting Dad back to work" was what really mattered to Americans. In the eyes of society, un-

less a woman was single and self-supporting, she was supposed to be a homemaker, helping her family through the national crisis by being thrifty and resourceful. Yet, it was the marginal wages brought home by many wives that kept some families going.

Some women took part-time jobs, but even then could rarely make enough to make ends meet, especially if they had to pay for streetcars or buses to get to work or to buy work clothes. Those who did work outside the home were often ostracized for taking work away from a man.

Children of unemployed parents would often drop out of high school or even junior high to get jobs to help meet family expenses. Even many of those who stayed in school got part-time jobs like paper routes to bring in extra money. But like other kinds of employment, these jobs were scarce, and the dads got first priority.

Whatever their age, gender, or education level, millions of unemployed Americans were on the brink of despair. In a haunting note left just before he jumped to his death from the George Washington Bridge, an unemployed Polish artist from Greenwich Village wrote: "To All: If you cannot hear the cry of

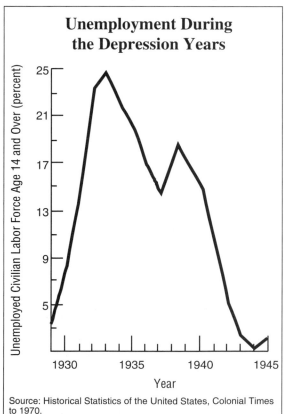

Unemployment During the Depression Years

Unemployed Civilian Labor Force Age 14 and Over (percent)

25
21
17
13
9
5

1930   1935   1940   1945

Year

Source: Historical Statistics of the United States, Colonial Times to 1970.

starving millions, listen to the dead, brothers. Your economic system is dead." [12]

Even the rich felt anxious and helpless. Steel magnate Charles M. Schwab had millions of dollars and an expensive Manhattan townhouse, yet he freely confessed: "I'm afraid. Every man is afraid." Marriner Eccles, a wealthy banker who had made it through the stock market crash with his fortune intact, wrote: "I awoke to find myself at the bottom of a pit without any known means of scaling its sheer sides." [13]

New Deal Programs Bring Jobs to U.S. Cities

Only after Congress started to approve FDR's New Deal relief programs did unemployment figures start to go down. The Works Progress Administration (WPA) alone put over 3.5 million of the nation's jobless to work building more than 650,000 miles of roads, 800 airports, 150,000 schools and other buildings, and countless parks, dams, and other public projects.

Programs like the Public Works Administration, Civil Works Administration, and WPA employed people regardless of their education level or prior

Families who were evicted from their homes and apartments often had to live in "shantyvilles" of tents and tarpaper shacks that offered little shelter from cold and storms.

work experience. When Frank C. Walker, an attorney and one of the executives appointed by FDR to coordinate the various works programs, toured his home state of Montana, he reported, "I saw old friends of mine—men I had been to school with—digging ditches and laying sewer pipe. They were wearing their regular business suits as they worked because they couldn't afford overalls and rubber boots." [14]

As he toured the country, Walker met a man who said,

I hate to think what would have happened if this work hadn't come along. The last of my savings had run out. I'd sold or hocked everything I could. And my kids were hungry. I stood in front of the window of the bake shop down the street and I wondered just how long it would be before I got desperate enough to pick up a rock and heave it through that window and grab some bread to take home.[15]

Because job prospects during the depths of the depression were especially poor for younger people in the nation's cities, the president set up the Civilian Conservation Corps (CCC) to give 2.5 million men between the ages of seventeen and twenty-eight jobs in city, state, and federal parks planting trees, fighting forest fires, caring for wildlife, making trails, and building reservoirs.

Each CCC enlistee received free transportation to his assigned camp and free medical care, and was issued

The New Deal's Civil Conservation Corps provided many young men with work maintaining park buildings and grounds. Here a group is thinning a stand of Scotch pine in a state park in Pennsylvania. In addition to a small salary, the men received room and board.

free work clothing, blankets, and a mess kit. He worked hard, from morning to night, for $30 a month (plus free room and board). Of that, he was allowed to keep only $5; the rest was sent home to his parents.

For some, it was the first time they had ever been out of the city. One New York boy who had been sent to a forest in Utah describes building an entire camp from scratch: "We chopped trees and built cabins and even a mess hall. For the next three years I grew up, physically, mentally, and spiritually, in that beautiful country. It was one of the most rewarding experiences of my life."[16]

The work was hard and the salaries low in all the New Deal work relief programs, but for families who had not had enough money coming in to adequately feed their children, these programs were a godsend.

Putting Food on the Table

After finding a job, the number-one priority of the poor in the early thirties was their next meal. There were no federal relief, unemployment insurance, or welfare programs to fall back on. As hundreds of thousands of people began losing their jobs and

running out of money for food, local municipal governments and charitable organizations like the Salvation Army began sponsoring breadlines in the nation's cities. In February 1930 breadlines in New York's Bowery district alone were feeding over two thousand people a day. Soon after that, many cities opened municipal soup kitchens.

But even breadlines and soup kitchens weren't enough. Every day mobs of hungry people would ransack city garbage dumps in hopes of finding

Before FDR's New Deal programs, the Red Cross and other charities set up volunteer shelters such as this homeless men's shelter in Sioux City, Iowa, to help cope with the overwhelming numbers of hungry and homeless people.

discarded scraps of food. Some were bolder. In January 1931, the *New York Times* reported an incident in Oklahoma City the day before:

A crowd of men and women, shouting that they were hungry and jobless, raided a grocery store near the City Hall today. Twenty-six of the men were arrested. Scores loitered near the city jail following the arrests, but kept well out of range of fire hose made ready for use in case of another disturbance.[17]

Even in homes with a steady income, parents constantly struggled to feed their families nutritious, appetizing meals on pennies a day. They relied on staples like flour, lard, beans, onions, potatoes, and rice. Cookbook author Darlene Campbell recalls how her mother used little more than flour, milk, an onion, and potatoes to create such appetizing meals as pancakes for breakfast, biscuits and gravy for lunch, and cream of potato soup with dumplings for dinner: "During a period of unemployment, we didn't know how long it would be until we'd see a regular paycheck again, so we went to a store that sells food in bulk. We purchased ten-pound sacks of rice and beans, among other items."[18]

The cost of a pound of butter in June 1930 was 54 cents; coffee was 29 cents a pound, prime rib 35 cents, and fresh eggs 35 cents a dozen. Meat was a luxury; so were fresh fruit and vegetables beyond those that came from a family's own garden. Since family gardens were a virtual necessity, another of a mother's jobs was to can and preserve as much of the surplus produce as possible for the winter months.

Malnutrition was a serious problem. In 1933, Manhattan's Children's Bureau reported that one out of every five children was not getting enough to eat. When food became scarce, many women in unemployed families had to send their children to live with relatives or friends.

Writer Louis Adamic recalls how he and his wife answered the door of their New York City apartment early one cold January morning in 1932 to find a young girl and boy in thin, patched clothing carrying schoolbooks:

In a voice strangely old for her age, the girl said: "Excuse me, mister, but we have no eats in our house and my mother she said I should take my brother before we go to school and ring a doorbell in some house . . . and ask you to give us something to eat."[19]

The story he told was not an uncommon one. A little girl in a coal-mining town was asked by her teacher whether she was ill. She responded, "No, I'm all right. I'm just hungry."

When the teacher suggested she go home and eat something, the girl said, "I can't. This is my sister's day to eat."[20]

In 1931, hospitals in New York City reported 95 deaths from starvation, while an additional 110 people (most of them children) died of malnutrition.

At the same time Congress was enacting New Deal programs to provide jobs for the unemployed, it created the Federal Emergency Relief Administration to grant $500 million to state governments to provide direct and immediate relief to people needing necessities such as food and shelter. Individual state governments decided how to distribute the money.

Thousands of Families Lose Their Homes

After food, the next most pressing concern for the unemployed poor was shelter. Referring to the need for early New Deal legislation, President Roosevelt said:

> One of the major disasters of the continued depression was the loss of hundreds of thousands of homes each year from foreclosure. By 1932, 273,000 families had lost their homes because they could no longer make the monthly mortgage payments. By the middle of 1933, foreclosures had advanced to more than 1,000 per day.[21]

Not only homeowners were thrown out into the cold; millions of tenants were evicted by their landlords when they couldn't meet the rent. Many families were even forced to leave their furniture behind because they had bought it on the installment plan and were unable to keep up those payments.

Where did all these homeless families go? Some were lucky enough to have relatives that could take them in. Others were forced to move to crowded, low-rent tenement slums or to makeshift shacks they built out of scrap lumber and tarpaper on abandoned lots on the outskirts of town. With nothing but open fires to keep them warm during the winter months, people wadded up newspaper under their clothes and stuffed it into their shoes to ward off the cold. It was not uncommon to see homeless men sleeping in subway stations or on park benches.

During FDR's first one hundred days in office, Congress passed the Homeowners' Loan Act, which authorized the federal government to refinance personal mortgages. The act provided that the holder of a defaulted mortgage could turn it over to the government in exchange for a guaranteed government bond. This protected the homeowner from losing his home while at the same time guaranteeing that the original mortgage issuer would be paid.

The Cost of Living for an Average Family

The average annual family income fell drastically in the early years of the depression from about $2,300 a year in 1929 to $1,600 or less in 1932. According to the Bureau of Labor Statistics, by 1935 the average middle-class family consisted of 2 adults and 1.6 kids living in a four- or five-room rented house or apartment on a gross annual income of $1,348. Only 3 percent of families owned their own homes and renters often offered to do a lot of the repairs themselves to help hold down the rent. The basic necessities—food, shelter, and clothing—consumed at least three-quarters of the average family's budget.

Thousands of homeless New York families were forced to move to low-rent tenement slums that were already overcrowded with blacks and immigrants.

The March Against Polio

By the time of the Great Depression, polio (paralytic poliomyelitis) was perhaps the most feared disease known. Polio struck suddenly, lacked a cure, and crippled its victims for life. Hobbling on crutches, rolling in wheelchairs, or lying immobile in giant iron lungs, the number of sufferers increased from year to year.

Franklin Delano Roosevelt fell ill with the disease in 1921 (at the age of thirty-eight) and never walked unaided again. He turned his private misfortune into a public fight against the disease that blossomed into the most successful medical fund-raising campaign ever mounted. By the time FDR came down with the disease, 27,363 cases had been reported nationally, including 7,179 deaths. The most concentrated outbreak of polio occurred in New York City. It was as though a medieval plague had returned; no one really knew how it was transmitted. Quack remedies abounded. Frog's blood, radium water, mustard plaster, wine of pepsin, a drink made of rum, brandy, and champagne—all these were touted as cures. Even fresh ox blood was offered as a treatment, prompting people to show up at slaughterhouses with empty buckets. All of it was futile. Anyone anywhere could become the next victim to suffer the headaches, fever, and muscle pains that led to paralysis or death. Roosevelt declared a war on polio during his administration, calling for the development of a polio vaccine, but it still took years of intense and costly research until the early 1960s when the Salk and Sabin vaccines proved successful.

In 1933 one of Roosevelt's supporters came up with the idea of holding nationwide public dances, or birthday balls, to celebrate the president's birthday, with the money raised to go to polio research. After four years of these fund-raisers an FDR aide came up with a new, even better idea. He suggested that national radio programs donate a half-minute of time to "ask the people to send their dimes directly to the President at the White House. Think what a thrill the people would get. . . . And we could call it the March of Dimes!"

About one out of every two families owned an automobile, but chances were that it was an old car purchased in more prosperous times or a secondhand model bought for a couple hundred dollars and a do-it-yourself patch-up job. Because gasoline, tires and replacement parts were expensive, most people living in the city rode more cost-effective public transportation such as streetcars, trains, and buses.

Few people bought clothing unless it was absolutely necessary. (Men's suits sold for between $30 and $75, while an average pair of men's shoes went for $4.) Even families with an employed breadwinner had little extra cash to spend. "Doing without" was a fact of life for them, too. Some mothers made play clothes for their children out of flour sacks to save their other clothes, along with their shoes, for school and church. They mended, patched, and recycled hand-me-downs until they simply wore out.

Family Life in the Thirties

Parents rarely went anywhere without their children; if they did, the older children took care of the younger ones. Each child had specific chores and responsibilities such as helping with the washing, ironing, cooking, cleaning, or dressing and bathing the younger children.

Although the depression caused a lot of hardship for families, both working and not, people still found ways to have fun. Families listened to the radio together in the evenings or played games together. They went on picnics and camping trips, listened to baseball games and wrestling matches on the radio, and went to the movies. Often neighbors would get together to play cards or go on picnics.

Kids rode bicycles, played ball (even if they had to use a stick for a baseball bat), built soapbox cars that they raced in neighborhood derbies, and played with Shirley Temple dolls. One of the most popular forms of escapist entertainment for kids (and more than a few adults) was comic strips, especially Dick Tracy, Buck

During the depression, families listened to comedy and drama programs on the radio or played games together.

Rogers, Flash Gordon, Little Orphan Annie, and Tarzan.

At the same time, city kids grew up very aware of the fears and anxieties of their parents. A WPA writer in New York described kids in a typical Bronx neighborhood:

The youngsters who grew up in the long gorge of a street that is Grant Ave. are a tough, uncompromising lot, many of them taking hold of their problems in a realistic way. They talk a clipped, wisecracking language just about as soft as the pavement under their feet and energy and emotion goes into dancing, jitterbug stuff, although they will tell you that over in the East Bronx, the sharpies have it all over them when it comes to dancing. The kids play ball in the street, skip rope. . . . The neighborhood is all buildings, red, tan, gray and rising sheer and flat off the street. . . . This community . . . has gotten a little frayed around the edges and battered in the middle as if the muddy waters that run down from the Concourse when it rains have seeped into the cellars and plumbing of the houses so that the people drink muddy water, and maybe that makes them so gray and gloomy.[22]

Questionable Solutions

Terrible times don't always make people sympathetic to their fellow man. Blacks and other minorities were hit harder by unemployment because they were almost always the last to be hired and the first to be fired. Yet many other Americans saw them as a cause of the unemployment problem, not the victims of it.

Mississippi governor Theodore Bilbo declared that the unemployment problem could be easily solved by simply shipping America's 12 million blacks to Africa. The veterans of the 1936 Spanish War were another group with a solution: They demanded the deportation of 10 million legal resident aliens so that more paychecks could go to "real" Americans. (Never mind that there were actually only 4 million aliens in the country at the time.) In fact, many noncitizens who were unable to find work *did* leave, voluntarily returning to their homelands. In 1932, more than three times as many people left the country as entered it.

Prejudice did not stop with African Americans and aliens. Several women's magazines actually suggested that working women could help solve the depression by giving men their jobs. And a retired major seriously recommended killing the nation's old people who were "of no use to themselves or anyone else."

The depression was harder on older Americans, especially those who did not have enough money to live on their own but were reluctant to burden their children, who were often just barely able to keep their own families afloat. Many suffered from job-related injuries or chronic disabling conditions (like deafness or black lung disease). Before Social Security became law in the mid-1930s, few people had any sort of safety net to fall back on when they got older. Very few had pensions or health insurance.

Although many older people suffered through the depression in pain and poverty and husbands sometimes deserted their families when they were unable to find work, just as many American families stuck together and in some way helped each other survive the fear and despair of the 1930s. When they describe this period to their children and grandchildren, many will also insist that the depression made them stronger and more caring people.

Author Tillie Olsen vividly describes her experiences as a young woman living in the city in the thirties—the degrading misery of hunger and despair, the labor violence, the homeless vagrants—yet, like so many other depression survivors, she came out of the experience with hope for the future:

> I live, too, with the beauty of the decade: its affirmation of democracy and action, . . . the still unseen evidence of human greatness in words, spirit and deed; the burgeoning solidarity in the nation, bridging differences in color, background, creed. . . . Out of that sense of identification came our first body of literature, art, songs, photographs, film. . . . For the first time, we began to have a sense of our country in all its hues, its wrongs and its rights, its unique diversity and likenesses, its pain.[23]

Chapter Two

As the land on the Great Plains dried up, the wind carried great black clouds of dust and sand, covering houses, roads, and farm animals in drifts of dirt. Soil drifts threatened to completely cover this farmer's home in Liberal, Kansas, in the summer of 1936.

Blowin' Down the Road

When farmers first settled on the southern plains at the turn of the twentieth century—the panhandles of Texas and Oklahoma, western Kansas, and the eastern portions of Colorado and New Mexico—it was a land lush with shrubs and grasses, with soil so rich some said it looked like chocolate. What they didn't realize was that the rainy years that made it so lush came in cycles that alternated with periods of severe drought. They also didn't realize what would happen when they plowed under the prairie grasses whose roots had held the topsoil in place and then planted and harvested crops year in and year out, without allowing the natural prairie grass to rest and replenish the soil. By the 1920s, many farmers were plowing with John Deere tractors instead of horses, allowing them to turn an average of fifty acres a day instead of two or three. All of their efforts went into making every inch of the plains produce maximum harvests.

A Long Dry Spell

But in the summer of 1931, the rains they had taken for granted stopped and their lush crops withered and died. Years of overplanting and overplowing had not only robbed the topsoil of nutrients but also made it harder for the soil to hold in moisture. A long dry spell meant disaster. The land became parched, the winds picked up, and the "black blizzards" started rolling in without warning, blotting out the sun and casting entire towns into darkness.

Powerful dust storms with gale-force winds blowing sixty to seventy miles per hour carried millions of tons of stinging, blinding black dirt across the southern plains, sometimes as far east as Washington and other cities on the east coast. Topsoil that had taken thousands of years to build up was blown away in minutes. Robert Geiger, a journalist for the *Washington Evening Star,* traveled through the plains after the first dust storm hit and gave the devastated region its name: He called it the "dust bowl." But it was

not just the panhandles of Texas and Oklahoma, western Kansas, and the eastern portions of Colorado and New Mexico that were affected. From 1933 to 1936, twenty plains states set records for dryness, many of which still stand today.

Lawrence Svobida, a wheat farmer from Kansas who later published a book about his depression experiences called *An Empire of Dust,* describes how he could see an approaching dust storm when it was still miles away:

Already it has the banked appearance of a cumulus cloud, but it is black instead of white, and it hangs low, seeming to hug the earth. Instead of being slow to change its form, it appears to be rolling on itself from the crest downward. As it sweeps onward, the landscape is progressively blotted out. Birds fly in terror before the storm, and only those that are strong of wing may escape. The smaller birds fly until they are exhausted, then fall to the ground, to share the fate of the thousands of jack rabbits which perish from suffocation.[24]

Often after the winds of a dust storm subsided, an eerie orange curtain of dust would hang over the landscape. People emerging from their houses would find dead or dying dirt-choked livestock lining the roads or buried under huge drifts of sand along with their tractors and other equipment.

In 1932 the weather bureau reported fourteen dust storms. The next year, the number climbed to thirty-eight. Yet through it all, the farmers kept plowing and sowing wheat because they believed it just had to start raining again soon. But it didn't, and by 1934, the storms were coming with even more alarming frequency.

How Bad Was the Dust?

Kansas resident Imogene Glover recalls:

The farmhouses looked terrible— the dust was deposited clear up to the window sills in these farmhouses, clear up to the window sills. And even about half of the front door was blocked by this sand. And if people inside wanted to get out, they had to climb out through the window to get out with a shovel to shovel out the front door. And, ah, there was no longer any yard at all there, not a green sprig, not a living thing of any kind, not even a field mouse. Nothing.[25]

Another survivor remembers, "When those dust storms blew and you were out in 'em well you spit out dirt. It looked like tobacco juice only it was dirt."[26]

Gene Howe, the publisher of a newspaper in Amarillo, Texas, counted twenty-seven days out of thirty in April 1935 when the dust was so thick he could not see across the street. Melt White recalls:

In the spring of 1935 the wind blew 27 days and nights without quittin', and I remember that's why my mother just—I thought she was going to go crazy because it was just— it was—you got desperate, because if the wind blew durin' the day or durin' the night and let up, you got some relief. But just day and night, 24 hours, one 24-hour after the other, it just—but it's 27 days and nights in the spring of 1935 it didn't let up.[27]

Much of everyone's day was spent trying to keep up with the dirt as it piled up. Rising early, women checked to make sure the rags and gummed tape stuffed under doorsills and on window ledges were still snug and blocking out the breeze. They replaced bedsheets suspended from the ceilings to trap floating dirt. Even attics had to be swept to prevent ceilings from caving in from the weight of dirt.

In spite of their best efforts, the dirt was everywhere. Writer Ann Marie Low describes the losing battle she and her mother fought every day:

Mama couldn't make bread until I carried water to wash the bread mixer. I couldn't churn until the churn was washed and scalded. We just couldn't do anything until something was washed first. Laundry day was especially demanding. I had to wash out the boiler, wash tubs, and the washing machine before we could use them. Then every towel, piece of bedding, and garment had to be taken out doors to have as much dust as possible shaken out before washing.[28]

What made the fight against dirt even more demanding was that most farms had no modern washers, running water, or bathrooms, so women not only had to wash clothes by hand, they had to haul water from the well with buckets first and then heat it over a wood-burning stove. Most even made their own soap first by boiling lye. To make a fire, women used cow chips as their primary source of fuel. (If people were fortunate enough to have corn cobs they used those for heating and cooking; only rarely did people have enough money for coal and the scarcity of trees on the plains

Dust storms in Oklahoma usually arrived suddenly in the form of an advancing wall of dust and debris that was often miles long and several thousand feet high. They struck with little warning, making driving conditions hazardous.

limited the amount of wood available for fuel.)

At night, mothers covered cribs with cloths to prevent babies from breathing in dirt and suffocating in their sleep. They gave older children damp rags to cover their mouths while they slept and shook out bedclothes in futile attempts to make beds sand-free.

Woody Guthrie's Talking Dust Bowl Blues

Woody Guthrie lived in Pampa in the Texas panhandle when the dust storms were at their worst. He wrote both "The Great Dust Storm" and "Dusty Old Dust (So Long It's Been Good to Know Yuh)" about the great Black Sunday storm.

Back in nineteen twenty seven
I had a little farm and I called it heaven
Prices up and the rain come down
I hauled my crops all into town
Got the money . . . bought clothes and
    groceries . . .
Fed the kids . . . and raised a big family
But the rain quit and the wind got high
Black old dust storm filled the sky
I traded my farm for a Ford machine
Poured it full of this gas-i-line
And started . . . rocking and a-rolling
Deserts and mountains . . . to California
Way up yonder on a mountain road
Hot motor and a heavy load
Going purty fast, wasn't even stopping
Bouncing up and down like popcorn a-
    popping
Had a breakdown . . . kind of a nervous
    bustdown
Mechanic feller there charged me five
    bucks
And said it was En-gine trouble
Way up yonder on a mountain curve
Way up yonder in a piney wood
I gave that rolling Ford a shove
Gonna coast just fars as I could
Commence a rolling . . . picking up speed
Come a hairpin turn . . . and I didn't make it
Man alive, I'm a telling you
The fiddles and guitars really flew
That Ford took off like a flying squirrel
Flew halfway around the world
Scattered wives and children
All over the side of that mountain
Got to California so dad-gum broke
So dad-gum hungry I thought I'd choke

Woody Guthrie (1912–1967) was an American songwriter and folksinger raised in the Texas Panhandle where the dust storms were at their worst.

I bummed up a spud or two
Wife fixed up some tater stew
We poured the kids full of it
Looked like a tribe of thy-mometers
    arunning around
Lord, man, I swear to you
That was surely mighty thin stew
So damn thin I really mean
You could read a magizine
Right through it . . . look at the pictures too
Purty whiskey bottles . . . naked women
Always have thought, always figured
If that damn stew had been a little thinner
Some of these here politicians
Could of seen through it.

Grasshoppers and Jackrabbits

The dry weather of the dust bowl thirties may have been devastating to crops, farm animals, and humans, but it was great for grasshoppers, especially from 1930 to 1935, when the drought was most severe. Vast swarms of grasshoppers (also called locusts) could blot out the sun. When a swarm descended on a farm, not only did it destroy what little crops there were, it took every leaf off the trees and devour every blade of grass, every vegetable and flower in the gardens, leaving the ground practically bare. A South Dakota woman remembers:

> Migrating hordes of grasshoppers descended so thick you couldn't see the sides of buildings. Fence posts were twice their normal size with grasshoppers, and highways were slushy and slick. As soon as they hit the ground they headed for the tree and started up it and began to eat the leaves. The next morning they had eaten every leaf, and there were a lot of hoppers eating the young branches. It didn't take very long and they killed the tree.[29]

Grasshoppers weren't the only infestation farmers had to deal with. In 1935, after years of drought and dust, hundreds of thousands of starving jackrabbits came down from the hills, devouring everything in their path, forcing farmers to begin an extermination campaign. Dust bowl farmer J. R. Davidson said jackrabbits were so thick that from a distance they appeared to be herds of sheep:

> The first rabbit drive that I ever witnessed was with shotguns, but that was kind of dangerous, so then they decided later that they'd have some more of these rabbit drives, and we'd just use clubs. So they would form lines of people, and these lines of people would march down through that country and come together, and funnel these rabbits into those pens, and any that tried to get back by you, which would be a lot of 'em, why you were supposed to knock them in the head with the club as they came by. And then after they got them all in these pens, why, the young fellows would get in those pens with these clubs, which was like an old axe handle or something like this, and—and just club them to death.[30]

Farming Was a Hard Life

The drought was made worse by some of the hottest summers on record. Deep wells with windmills provided drinking water, but not enough extra

Rural children such as this New Jersey girl worked hard both before and after school helping out their parents with farm chores.

make it to safety in time, and suffocate. They had reason to fear; dust storms could kill. To make sure they could make it back to the house after milking the cows, some farmers strung clothesline out to the barn.

Crops were ruined. As Lawrence Svobida writes:

> When I knew that my crop was irrevocably gone I experienced a deathly feeling which, I hope, can affect a man only once in a lifetime. My dreams and ambitions had been flouted by nature, and my shattered ideals seemed gone forever. The very desire to make a success of my life was gone; the spirit and urge to strive were dead within me. Fate had dealt me a cruel blow above which I felt utterly unable to rise.[31]

Wives shared their husbands' despair. Women shouldered child rearing and household chores like cooking, cleaning, washing, and ironing, but considerable responsibility for farm chores like milking cows and helping in the fields as well.

Even children shared the back-

to irrigate the bone-dry fields. Most farmers kept on plowing, somehow still optimistic year after year that the rains would return. What little wheat managed to sprout either soon turned brown and died or was eaten by grasshoppers or jackrabbits. The wives and children of these farmers would worry that the men would be caught out in a dust storm, unable to

breaking work and the deepening despair. Most rural children had farm chores to do before they left for school in the mornings such as feeding, watering, and milking. They were also expected to help with household chores and with feeding and dressing the younger children. There were no school buses in rural areas in the thirties so children often had to walk miles to and from school every day. This was a particular hardship in winter because most parents couldn't afford to buy their children boots and adequate warm clothing.

Rural schools were usually lit with kerosene lamps and heated when fuel was available by wood stoves. Attendance was so small in many sparsely populated rural areas that a number of grades usually filled up a single classroom. During recess in good weather, students played outside games like baseball, kick the can, hide and seek, jump rope, tag, treasure hunt, and marbles.

Keeping Spirits Up

Farming families who survived the "dirty thirties" remember terrible times, but most also remember that through it all, families still made their own fun. Neighbors threw barn dances and house parties with live fiddle and banjo music. Warmer weather

meant family picnics; sometimes in fall, families would go pheasant hunting together, with the dad and older sons doing the hunting while the mother and the daughters and younger sons rode along as "spotters."

In winter, families played cards or took turns hosting ice skating and sledding parties. Churches and clubs like 4-H sponsored many of these kinds of activities for both adults and children.

Farm Prices Plunge

As the devastation wrought by the drought and grasshopper infestations worsened, crops failed and cattle and other farm animals sickened and died. As a result, farm income fell drastically. Extremes of heat and cold only made matters worse. Cattle prices, which had previously been a stable source of income, fell so low that many farmers only kept enough cattle to feed themselves. Eventually, the only feed many farmers could provide for their animals was chopped up thistles, and the cattle slowly died of starvation.

Farm prices for plains farmers dropped to a drastic low: butterfat $.03 a pound, eggs $.02–$.03 a dozen, hogs $.02–$.03 a pound. "For a farmer to buy a toothbrush," said John A. Simpson, president of the National Farmers

Union, "he would have to sell eight dozen eggs and he then would owe two cents. A farmer must sell forty pounds of cotton to buy a good shirt."[32] The more the farmer produced and carried to market, the lower prices fell.

A South Dakota judge remembers: Many of them came by the courthouse. And they'd come by and see me and say, "Judge, you know, we've reached the end of our rope. We don't have anything left. We've got to get out of here." They were gaunt, tired-looking people. I felt very sorry for 'em. The whole family, the wife, the kids and the husband, they were tired-lookin' people, people that you could see felt rather hopeless.[33]

Heading for California

By the end of 1935, with no substantial rainfall in four years, many farming families simply gave up and headed west in search of farm jobs in California. (Californians disparagingly called them all Okies, even though only some of them

In 1930, drought struck, leaving already poor sharecroppers and tenant farmers without enough food or money to make it through the winter. Many packed up their family belongings and headed for California looking for work.

were actually from Oklahoma.) Some left because the bank foreclosed on their mortgages and seized their property.

Whole families packed their meager belongings onto old jalopies and didn't even bother to shut the door behind them. They just drove away. Banks and businesses failed, churches shut their doors, schools were boarded up.

Cleo Frost was eighteen years old in 1934 when she and her family left their Sallisaw, Oklahoma, home, bound for California: "There were 16 of us, including four young children. My brother bought a Chevrolet truck in Tulsa. We put blankets in the center for the kids to sleep on."[34]

Ed Holderby recalls his family's trip west:

> I recall quite vividly living in a tent at Fort Hall, Idaho, over the 4th of July, and eating only potatoes (scrubs and scraps gleaned from behind the digger) for 24 straight days. On the 24th day, my eldest brother Jim worked from 7 AM to noon loading sacks of potatoes into boxcars, which earned him 10 cents, with which he purchased a loaf of bread. My mother and my 10-year-old sister, Rosemary, played games like, "Who can

Heading West on Route 66

As John Steinbeck wrote in *The Grapes of Wrath:* "The dispossessed were drawn west from Kansas, Oklahoma, Texas, New Mexico; from Nevada and Arkansas, families, tribes, dusted out, tractored out. Carloads, caravans, homeless and hungry; twenty thousand and fifty thousand and a hundred thousand and two hundred thousand. They streamed over the mountains, hungry and restless—restless as ants, scurrying to find work to do—to lift, to push, to pull, to pick, to cut—anything, any burden to bear, for food. The kids are hungry. We got no place to live. Like ants scurrying for work, for food, and most of all for land."

For many of these destitute travelers, the road west was Highway 66. Steinbeck proclaimed Highway 66 the "Mother Road." While it was certainly a road to opportunity in the minds of the more than 200,000 who used the route to escape the despair of the dust bowl in search of golden California, Route 66 actually became more important to the farmers who stayed in the ravaged dust bowl of Kansas, Oklahoma, West Texas, and New Mexico. Paving the highway and improving its waysides became one of the main projects of both the New Deal's Civilian Conservation Corps (CCC) and Works Progress Administration (WPA). Starting in 1933, thousands of unemployed men were put to work as laborers on road gangs. As a result of this monumental effort, the Chicago-to-Los-Angeles highway was reported as "continuously paved" in 1938.

This movie still is taken from the movie The Grapes of Wrath, *based on John Steinbeck's classic novel about dust bowl sharecroppers heading for California. The 1940 movie was directed by John Ford and starred Henry Fonda, Jane Darwell, and John Carradine.*

come up with a brand new way to cook potatoes?" [35]

The New Deal Offers Hope

Although FDR did not immediately acknowledge the urgency of the farmers' plight, certain individuals within his administration believed that the health of the nation's farmers benefited the nation as a whole and worked to create farm aid programs. During the critical five-year period between 1932 and 1937, the Department of Agriculture (USDA) developed programs to improve rural credit facilities, awareness of the need for soil conservation measures, aid for poverty-stricken farmers to acquire farms, and loans for rural electrification. These programs led in turn to new agencies responsible for their administration. USDA's staff during these years increased from 27,000 to 106,000.

One of the first congressional New Deal acts to help farmers was the Agricultural Adjustment Act of 1933, which set up a direct financial relief program for eligible farmers. It also marked the beginning of government price supports for farm products. In 1933, Congress also passed the Emergency Farm Mortage Act to provide funds for refinancing farm mortages, and in 1935, it passed the Resettlement Administration Act, which helped resettle destitute farmers on better land.

There were people who had seen the disasters of the dust bowl coming. Hugh Hammond Bennett, who would come to be known as the father of soil conservation, led a campaign to reform farming practices with the intention of preserving the soil well before Roosevelt became president. By the midthirties Bennett was advising the Roosevelt administration that "Americans have been the greatest destroyers of land of any race or people,

barbaric or civilized."[36] He called for an all-out national effort to improve agricultural practices. Bennett wasn't criticizing dust bowl farmers as much as he was urging them to make changes in the way they farmed to avoid similar catastrophes in the future.

Bennett's problem was convincing Congress of the urgency of helping dust bowl farmers. In April 1935, he was on his way to testify before a congressional committee when he learned

Labor camps were set up in California in the 1930s to provide housing for "Okies," the sharecroppers and tenant farmers who were escaping the ravages of the dust bowl. The living conditions the newcomers faced were often worse than those they left behind.

of a dust storm blowing all the way east into Washington, D.C., from the western plains. The timing was perfect. Just as he was making his speech in front of a congressional committee, a dusty gloom settled over the nation's capital and blotted out the midday sun. In the dim light of the Senate chamber, Bennett exclaimed, "This, gentlemen, is what I have been talking about."[37] Congress responded by passing the Soil Conservation Act of 1935, a bill which authorized the government to pay farmers a dollar an acre to plant fewer soil-depleting crops and to employ other active soil conservation measures, such as planting fields with clover and other grasses every other year to replenish nutrients and prevent topsoil erosion.

Rural Electrification

A New Deal program that had one of the most dramatic and lasting impacts on rural America was the push for rural electrification. As late as the mid-1930s, nine out of ten rural homes were without electric service and living and working standards were primitive compared with life and work in the cities. Without electricity, agriculture was almost exclusively the only industry.

The private, investor-owned power companies that served most of the nation's cities did gradually extend their lines along many of the main roads leading out into the countryside, and some of the farmers who lived along those routes were able to take advantage of the central station electric service. But in those few and favored locations, the price of electricity was high and service often erratic. Rural customers were required to pay the full cost of connecting their homes to the "highline," a price ranging from $2,000 to $3,000 a mile.

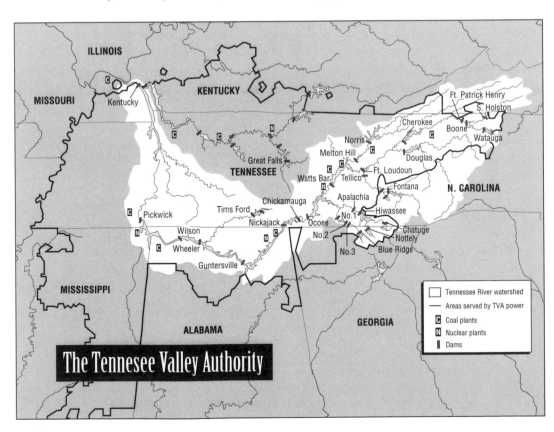

The Tennessee Valley Authority

(In 1998 dollars, this would be about $26,000 to $35,000.) And after the farmer paid to have a line extended to his home, that line became the property of the power company.

In the 1930s the New Deal legislation known as the Rural Electrification Act made it possible for many farming communities to form partnerships with an agency of the U.S. government to plan a network of not-for-profit electric cooperatives that would provide a source for reliable and cost-efficient electric service for all rural areas of the United States.

The first official action of the REA was the passage of the Tennessee Valley Authority Act in May 1933. The cost of building electric lines was generally estimated at between $1,500 and $2,000 per mile at the time the rural electrification program got underway. REA engineers designed more cost-effective ways to string electric lines and boost voltage, and even came up with the ingenious idea of having customers read their own meters.

By the end of World War II, 98 percent of the farms in the United States had electricity.

Other New Deal Programs Helped Rural America

The Farm Credit Association (FCA) was set up in the 1930s as an independent federal agency to supervise a network of cooperatively owned banks to issue loans to farmers, ranchers, commercial fishermen, and rural utility co-ops. In 1937, FDR's New Deal took farm credit a step further when Congress authorized the Farm Security Administration to lend money to sharecroppers and tenant farmers to help them buy their own farms.

Two of the projects funded by the WPA were the Hoover Dam and power plant. They were constructed to control the floods of the Colorado River, improve navigation of the river, and reclaim public lands to generate electrical energy.

Other New Deal programs and organizations that helped meet the needs of dust bowl residents were the Federal Emergency Relief Administration, the Federal Surplus Relief Corporation, the Works Progress Administration, the Civilian Conservation Corps, and the Drought Relief Service.

Work Programs Supplement Income

Many farmers helped ends meet by finding work in a New Deal work program. They graveled roads and built schools, dams, and airports. Workers in the CCC created national and state parks and wildlife preserves. Teachers and other professionals repaired books at local libraries, served lunches at local schools, compiled state guides, and organized the manuscripts of hundreds of county archives.

To rural people who took great pride in their independence and self-sufficiency, relief measures during the Great Depression were often painful and humiliating; to be eligible for aid, the farmer often had to prove that he was too poor to even borrow the necessary money to purchase fuel and oil. Only then would he be given a credit slip entitling him to the supplies he needed most.

Nevertheless, most dust bowl farmers were immensely appreciative of Roosevelt and his New Deal programs. For many, only federal aid made it possible for them to wait out the blistering years of drought and dust.

When the rains finally came at the end of the decade and the Great Plains could once again yield a bountiful harvest, the strong relationship between the farmer and the federal government, which still included a system of price supports and subsidies, remained.

The End of the Thirties in Rural America

The dust storms of the thirties had taught plains farmers hard lessons. When the drought cycle wound down in 1937, many farmers turned cropland into pastures and grassland. Others planted long shelterbelts of trees to break the wind and to hold the remaining topsoil. State colleges focused research on soil erosion. The federal government purchased millions of acres of farmland and turned it to grasslands, and continued to pay farmers to alternate years of crop planting with years of fallow, during which the soil could be replenished with clover or other grasses. Federal funds paid for more dams to help the soil retain moisture and to create electricity. Ultimately, the dust bowl made people realize that soil ecology was fragile and that they had to take measures and precautions to conserve it.

Chapter Three

Labor strikes to improve working conditions were a regular and often violent occurrence during the 1930s, when the idea of workers' rights came to the forefront.

Great Inroads for the Labor Movement

Although the Great Depression was disastrous for millions of American workers, it actually sparked a tremendous growth in the power of the labor movement as a whole. For the first time in the country's history, legislation was passed that guaranteed workers the right to bargain collectively for higher pay and better working conditions. But many workers in the '30s had to wage long and bitter strikes to win their demands, often in spite of government guarantees. Meanwhile, the Communist and Socialist Parties used labor unrest to push their anticapitalist ideologies and gain political clout while unscrupulous politicians like Senator Huey Long exploited the labor movement for personal power.

Labor Loses Ground in the 1920s

During the previous decade, corporate America had blossomed into the era of big business. Between 1919 and 1929, over twelve hundred mergers swallowed up more than six thousand previously independent companies. By 1929, two hundred corporations controlled almost 50 percent of all American industry. While labor productivity increased by an astonishing 43 percent during the prosperous 1920s, wages increased only slowly during the same period, nowhere near the rate of production. As a consequence, more and more American workers could not afford to buy what they produced. Unions were not much help. The AFL (American Federation of Labor) under Samuel Gompers consisted mainly of craft unions; unskilled industrial workers were still largely unorganized.

Workers Promised a New Deal

Franklin D. Roosevelt won the presidential election in 1932 because he promised to address the problems of American workers, in both the long and short term. Economic recovery, he believed, was not enough; the depression had exposed great wrongs in the American system of capitalism that cried out for reform. He said, "These unhappy times call for the building of plans that rest upon . . . the forgotten man at the bottom of the pyramid. Every man has a right to life; and this means that he also has a right to make a comfortable living."[38]

In addition to relief programs designed to keep unemployed families from starving and guaranteed mortgage loans to keep them from losing their homes, Roosevelt proposed a public works program to increase employment by giving the jobless temporary work in the national forests, on flood-control projects, and on government construction projects.

But FDR's long-term goals for labor went much further. He wanted government to limit the number of hours a day and days a week that industries could require their employees to work. His campaign also advocated higher wages, compulsory unemployment insurance, and state old-age pensions:

> These three great objectives—the security of the home, the security of livelihood, and the security of social insurance—are, it seems to me, a minimum of the promise that we can offer to the American people. They constitute a right which belongs to every individual and every family willing to work.

FDR's New Deal not only helped labor's short-term goal of providing the jobless with work, it passed laws guaranteeing workers the right to negotiate for better wages, shorter work weeks, and employment benefits such as pensions and unemployment insurance.

They are the essential fulfillment of measures already taken toward relief, recovery and reconstruction. This seeking for a greater measure of welfare and happiness does not indicate a change in values. It is rather a return to values lost in the course of our economic development and expansion.[39]

Key to protecting workers was ensuring their right to unionize. When union leaders such as John L. Lewis of the United Mine Workers Association (UMWA) and Sidney Hillman of the Amalgamated Clothing Workers of America (ACWA) called for government protection of the rights of workers to organize and engage in collective bargaining, the liberals who dominated Congress after the elections of 1932 listened. They guaranteed workers these rights under the National Industrial Recovery Act (NIRA), passed in 1933. Although the primary purpose of the bill was to encourage national industrial recovery, to foster fair competition, and to create employment opportunities by allocating $3.3 billion for the construction of public projects through programs such as the Public Works Administration, the NIRA was also designed to balance the interests of business and labor. Section 7(a) specifically provided that employees have the right to organize and bargain collectively through representatives of their own choosing, and that they shall be free from the interference, restraint, or coercion of their employers (or their employer's agents) while doing so. But corporate management found an ingenious way to get around the NIRA's provisions: They set up their own "company unions" in an effort to keep out those that workers wanted to organize independently. To be hired, a new employee had to agree to join the company union. When that didn't stop workers from organizing their own unions, many employers hired spies to report on union activities and armed guards to intimidate them.

Not until Congress passed the National Labor Relations Act in 1935 did protection of workers' bargaining rights actually start to be enforced. More commonly known as the Wagner Act, the National Labor Relations Act was not just a labor-union bill of rights; it was a specific list of what employers could not do, such as forcing employees to join company unions. It guaranteed labor's right to organize independently and made it illegal for employers to interfere with the process. It created an independent National Labor Relations Board to oversee elections and to hear complaints about unfair labor practices.

All of the "unfair practices" that the Wagner Act specified were practices that had been used by management; as far as the Wagner Act was concerned, there were no unfair labor practices used by unions. Thanks to the Wagner Act, union membership exploded in the last half of the 1930s, even while unemployment remained high. In 1934 union members comprised less than 12 percent of non-farmworkers and many of those were in company unions. By 1940 unions represented 26.9 percent.

A Number of New Labor Laws

A number of other important prolabor laws were passed in the thirties. In 1936, Congress passed the Anti-Strikebreaker Act (Byrnes Act), which declared it unlawful to transport or aid strikebreakers in interstate or foreign trade. It also established the Public Contracts Act (Walsh-Healey Act) to establish such labor standards as minimum wages, overtime pay, child and convict labor provisions, and safety standards on all federal contracts. In

The Death of Detroit Dreams

Before the stock market crash of October 1929, new car sales in the United States had hit a peak of 3,848,937 per year. They would not reach that level again for twenty years.

The crash hit the auto industry with incredible impact. People still had to eat, they still needed clothes, and they still needed shelter. But the purchase of a new car could usually be put off. In 1929, U.S. auto plants produced more than 5.5 million cars and trucks; by 1932, output fell to less than 1.4 million.

Many brand names fell by the wayside during the depression. Essex gave up in 1931, the Franklin disappeared in 1934, the Reo (Ransom E. Olds's second automotive venture) went under in 1936, joined by the Pierce Arrow in 1937. The Auburn Automobile Company of Auburn, Indiana, produced three American classics—the Auburn, the Cord, and the Duesenberg—all of which went out of production during the depression.

The "big three" survived the depression; in fact, GM made money every year and Chrysler actually grew. Ford Motor Company was wounded almost mortally, although nobody knew it because it was not a public company and its bookkeeping was terrible.

The poor economy of the '30s led to fierce competition in the auto industry, sparking innovations like airflow carburetors, front-wheel drive, V-8 engines, automatic transmissions, and turbochargers.

1937, Congress passed the National Apprenticeship Act, which established the Bureau of Apprenticeship within the Department of Labor, and in 1938, the Fair Labor Standards Act, which created a $.25 minimum wage and time-and-a-half pay for more than 40 hours per week.

A Long and Bloody Struggle

During the thirties, American employers may have lost the enormous power advantages they had enjoyed in the struggle over collective bargaining, but workers still had a hard and often bloody struggle to get employers to raise their wages and improve their working conditions. Job insecurity and anger over intolerable demands for production increases were two of the main grievances workers had. Bill Stinson describes the working conditions at a Ford plant in 1933 that eventually caused the workers to strike:

Until 1933 there were no rules: you were at the mercy of your foreman. I could go to work at seven o'clock in the morning and at seven fifteen the boss'd come around and say, you could come back at three o'clock. If he preferred somebody else over you, that person would be called back earlier, even though you were there longer. I left the plant so many nights hostile. It was lousy. Degraded. You might call yourself a man if you was on the street, but as soon as you went through the door you was nothing more or less than a robot.[40]

A turning point for labor occurred in 1934. The number of strikes more than doubled to 1,856 while the number of workers on strike increased fivefold, to 1,470,000, compared to the period 1929–1932. Strikes against management were a powerful tool for labor groups, but workers paid a high price in violence and lost wages. In Minneapolis, the Brotherhood of Teamsters staged a crippling strike against the city's transportation system to end a ban on unions. In retaliation, employers banded together and formed a "citizen's army" to oppose the strikers. In July, clashes killed two and wounded sixty-five, but the

The 1934 truck drivers' strike in Minneapolis was just one of many strikes American workers staged in their fight against employers in the midthirties. Their battle was not just for wage increases and improved conditions, but for the right to bargain collectively.

Teamsters had the support of the governor and eventually won the right for transportation workers to unionize.

A similar strike occurred in San Francisco the same year when longshoremen struck the docks, organizing a general city strike that eventually even shut down the city's small businesses. The strike ended in arbitration that not only granted the longshoremen the right to unionize, but actually won them most of their wage demands.

In the fall of 1934, 350,000 textile workers went on strike in the South, declining to accept policy from their own union leadership. Seven strikers were killed by police. Armed strikebreakers were hired by the company for use against the workers. However, the strike spread to Massachusetts and Rhode Island. By September, some 420,000 textile workers were on strike throughout the entire country.

Not all striking groups were that successful. Many could not hold out against the violence of opposing employers or live without incomes long enough to win the right to unionize.

A New, Effective Tactic: The Sit-Down Strike

During the Great Depression, employers tried to get as much work as possible from their employees for the lowest possible wage. One of labor's most effective tactics in the fight for higher wages and better working conditions turned out to be the sit-down strike, in which union members literally occupied the plant in which they were working. Instead of picketing outside the plant, the striking workers remained inside (sometimes for weeks and even months) until management gave in and agreed to their demands.

The sit-down was an effective way to strike. If workers struck a plant by walking off the job and picketing, management could bring in new workers (scabs) to break the strike. But if workers stayed in the plant, management could not so easily resume production. It also discouraged the use of violence against strikers, because deploying police, troops, or other armed groups against sit-downers risked destroying expensive company-owned buildings, machinery, and materials.

The UAW Strikes a Major Blow for American Workers

Seeking strength in unity, automobile workers from throughout the country joined forces to form the United Automobile Workers of America (UAW) in 1935. The union decided to fight the first battle against General Motors, the nation's largest industrial employer, with more than a quarter-million workers. Determined to avoid union-

During the 1930s workers and unionists invented the sit-down strike—a powerful and revolutionary weapon to bring industrial employers to the bargaining table. Instead of picketing, employees occupy their workplaces. This photo shows the first successful sit-down strike staged in 1937 by the United Auto Workers in Flint, Michigan.

ization at all costs, GM had spent close to $1 million between January 1934 and July 1936 to intimidate its workforce with what a U.S. Senate committee called "the most colossal super system of spies yet devised in any American corporation."[41]

Throughout November and December 1936, as the UAW leaders formulated their plans, autoworkers jumped the gun and began to stage sit-down strikes in South Bend, Kansas City, Detroit, Atlanta, and other cities.

Striking in Flint, Michigan, took a lot of courage because Flint was a virtual company town. The mayor, police chief, and three city commissioners, as well as Flint's newspaper, radio station, and school officials, all were or had been on the General Motors payroll. GM's Chevrolet, Buick, Fisher Body, and AC Spark Plug plants employed four of every five workers in the city.

After GM's attempt to get a court injunction to evict the strikers failed, the company turned to more drastic tactics. Company guards turned off the heat inside Chevrolet No. 2 plant (in 16-degree weather) and barred strike supporters from bringing in food. When sit-downers forced open the factory gates to allow the food in, GM called out the police. On January 11, sheriff's deputies and police, using tear gas, billy clubs, and guns, stormed the plant.

Strikers repelled the assault by turning on the plant's fire hoses and raining two-pound car hinges down on the police. Later that night the police returned and were driven back a second time. Humiliated and angry, the cops opened fire, wounding several strikers. A third police charge, at midnight, also failed. Defeated, the police (called "bulls" by the strikers) abandoned the field.

The next morning, nonstriking Flint workers lined up two abreast at UAW headquarters to sign membership cards and pay dues. Ten thousand people gathered at the battle site, repeatedly singing "Solidarity Forever," the labor anthem written by activist balladeer Joe Hill.

FDR Remains Silent

Under pressure from GM officials, Michigan governor Frank Murphy ordered fifteen hundred National Guardsmen into Flint and tried to talk the unionists into leaving the plants with the promise of negotiations. GM was unwilling to compromise, however. Company agents, police, and vigilantes beat UAW pickets and organizers not only in Flint but also in Detroit, Saginaw, and Anderson, Michigan, and in other auto plants where sit-down strikes inspired by events in Flint had spread. And though John L. Lewis called on President Roosevelt to help the workers, FDR remained silent. Roosevelt wanted a negotiated end to the strike and opposed using troops to evict the strikers, though he labeled the strikers' tactics wrong.

GM finally caved in. On February 13, with its car production at a near standstill, its share of the automobile market plummeting, and its tactics in Flint frustrated at every turn, General Motors agreed to negotiate. A week later, the company conceded defeat on the key issue of union recognition at its struck plants, acknowledged the UAW as bargaining agent for its members in those plants, and agreed not to organize company unions for six months. GM also agreed to drop all related lawsuits and to refrain from disciplining the strikers. All other UAW demands would be discussed in a national labor-management conference.

When Flint autoworkers beat General Motors—the largest producer of

"Populist" Huey Long

Communists weren't the only radicals to exploit labor issues for their own power gains. One of the most notable and powerful was Huey Long, a charismatic and controversial Louisiana governor who went on to be elected to the U.S. Senate in 1930. Technically a Democrat, Huey Long was actually a radical "populist" who championed the "little man" against the rich and privileged. (He gave himself the nickname "Kingfish" because, he said, "I'm a small fish here in Washington. But I'm the Kingfish to the folks down in Louisiana.")

As governor, he sponsored many reforms that endeared him to the rural poor. Four short years after becoming governor of Louisiana, he paved roads, built bridges, provided free textbooks to poor children, reformed the hospitals, broke the power of the old political bosses, and took on the near monopolistic power of the big oil companies. But it was how he used the power of his office that attracted attention: He ran the state as a veritable dictator, ignoring state constitutional laws and manipulating the state Democratic Party machine to get things done. He was so unscrupulous that within a year of taking office he was impeached by the Louisiana House of Representatives, although the charges were eventually dismissed by the state Senate.

While he was still governor in 1930, Long ran for and won a U.S. Senate seat, but what he really had his sights set on was the presidential race of 1932.

Many historians feel that if Long had not been assassinated in Baton Rouge, Louisiana, in 1935 (by the son of a man he had publicly criticized), he might have come close to achieving his ambitions—or

Senator Huey Pierce Long advocated a radical social program he called the Share-Our-Wealth Society. The society's slogan was "Every Man a King," and it promised homestead allowances of $6,500 and minimum annual incomes of $2,500 for each American household.

at least have made FDR's bid for reelection in 1936 much more difficult.

Most of the Americans who joined the Communist and socialist labor movements of the '30s and '40s were not, as their sometimes paranoid critics claimed, advocating the violent overthrow of the U.S. government; they had joined a party they felt would best help them protest the miserable working conditions and poor pay with which many American industrialists at the time were exploiting them. They wanted the right to organize so they'd have enough power to negotiate for better conditions. In fact, many of the New Deal programs FDR developed to pull the country out the Great Depression were criticized for being socialist.

automobiles, parts, and accessories in the world—their victory galvanized workers in auto and other basic industries all over the country. Their demands were extensive: a thirty-hour week, a six-hour day, and time-and-a-half pay for overtime so that work would be spread more widely; a minimum pay rate "commensurate with an American standard of living"; seniority based on length of employment (to limit management's arbitrary power) and reinstatement of "unjustly" fired employees; abolition of piecework; and establishment of joint control by management and the union over the speed of production in GM plants. To safeguard these and other gains from company and company-union tricks, the strikers demanded what the Wagner Act had only promised: recognition of the UAW as the "sole bargaining agency" for GM employees.

The Communist Party and the San Francisco General Strike

The Communist Party in the United States during the 1930s saw labor unrest as the way to gain strength in American society. Communists opposed capitalism as a system under which workers are exploited by wealthy industrialists. They believed that the ownership of industry was becoming concentrated in fewer and

fewer hands, plunging workers into a state of ever-increasing misery. They believed that the country's impoverished workers should rise up and organize themselves into a political party that would lead a revolution against the capitalists and take over ownership and management of the nation's industries. To many angry, underpaid, and overworked laborers, Communist promises sounded very appealing.

By 1934 the Communist Party had become more closely involved in waterfront unions, playing a crucial role in organizing and directing the San Francisco general strike in which 200,000 members of the International Longshoremen's Association (ILA) brought the coast's economy to a virtual standstill. In response, the National Recovery Act board stepped in and ordered the maritime employers to recognize the ILA union.

While the NRA action strengthened the ILA's position and helped its members challenge employers for higher wages and other benefits, many shippers were actually willing to suffer financial losses if it meant destroying the union. They refused to give in, setting the stage for bloody labor conflicts that eventually involved not only dock workers and employers, but the municipal government, city residents, and both local and state armed forces.

The Detroit Murals of Diego Rivera

In the '20s and '30s, industries in grimy, midwestern manufacturing cities like Chicago, Cleveland, and Pittsburgh started donating a small percentage of their profits to help beautify the cities with impressive art galleries and museums. The great car-making center of Detroit was no exception, although instead of filling its galleries with European art masterpieces, it decided to commission huge murals that would celebrate the city's industrial achievements.

By the 1920s, Detroit was already world famous as the home of the mass-production assembly line pioneered by the great American free-enterprise industrialist Henry Ford. So it was a little unusual when the Detroit Art Institute picked a Mexican communist to paint the "Detroit Industry" frescoes in 1933 instead of a local American artist. Not only that, but Henry Ford's son, Edsel, a director and patron of the Institute, was so impressed by Diego Rivera's preliminary sketches that he asked Rivera to paint not just two but all twenty-seven planned frescoes for $25,000.

Rivera spent nearly two months prior to the start of his work touring the motor city's car factories, sketching workers on the assembly lines, often in desperately hot and noisy conditions. He found his theme prowling odd corners of the city, visiting the neighborhoods of workmen's homes near the factories and the areas where ethnic groups' activities were centered. He saw Detroit, he said, as an expression of the steel that goes into automobiles and skyscrapers alike. On the

Renowned Mexican muralist Diego Rivera employed a simple style and colorful images to portray ordinary people.

walls of the Garden Court, he represented the four elements most important in the making of steel by four major female figures. "The yellow race represents the sand, because it is most numerous," he said. "And the red race, the first in this country, is like the iron ore, the first thing necessary for the steel. The black race is like coal, because it has a great native esthetic sense, a real flame of feeling and beauty in its ancient sculpture, its native rhythm and music. So its esthetic sense is like the fire, and its labor furnished the hardness which the carbon in the coal gives to steel. The white race is like the lime, not only because it is white, but because lime is the organizing agent in the making of steel. It binds together the other elements and so you see the white race as the great organizer of the world."

"Left Wing, Chicken Wing . . ."

In the midthirties, when he first reached California, Woody Guthrie went from singing about the plight of America's workers to singing about their banding together in unions to do something about it. This was also the beginning of his relationship with the American Communist Party.

After one of his radio shows, a friend of his who had caught some of the political undertones of his songs asked if he'd like to sing for a workers' rally. He told Woody he'd be sharing the stage with some Party members and some pretty strong left-wing folks. Woody's reputed response was, "Left wing, chicken wing, it don't make no difference to me." He would later play music at Communist Party gatherings and even write columns in Communist newspapers, but he always maintained that he was not a member of any "earthly organization." He was also quoted as saying, "I ain't a Communist necessarily, but I been in the red all my life."

Woody Guthrie is the original folk song hero. In the thirties and forties, he transformed the folk ballad into a vehicle for social protest and observation, literally writing hundreds of songs, such as "This Land Is Your Land," "So Long, It's Been Good to Know Yuh," and "Dust Bowl Refugees."

Between 1934 and 1940, San Francisco's police were controlled by antiunion business and political interests. Because most of the police force came from the same Catholic working-class backgrounds and neighborhoods as the union workers, Police Chief William Quinn and other antiunion politicians stressed that the enemy was not the workingman from the policeman's own neighborhood, but Communist infiltrators of the labor movement. By portraying communism as the enemy, they encouraged police officers to believe that when they crushed union strike attempts, they squashed the Communist threat to their way of life. Then antiunion municipal leaders hired more officers and armed them with more powerful firearms and chemical gases.

In San Francisco, attacks on suspected Communists began in earnest during the 1934 general strike. Business leaders used the threat of communism to deflect attention from labor issues which might have been negotiated to the benefit of workers. By branding strikes "Communist-inspired," employers did not have to negotiate in good faith with the unions, the mayor did not have to support the workers in negotiations, and the city government used all the police and arms necessary to crush strikes forcefully rather than seek negotiated settlements. The success of the San Francisco general strike inspired union militants across the nation. In part because the Communist Party performed a vital role in leading the strike, it became the dominant force on the left wing of the labor movement. The Communists, however, would be disappointed. The 1934 strike wave was not the beginning of a Communist or even Socialist revolution. The strikers' main objective had been winning union recognition, not inciting a nationwide or worldwide class revolution, and New Deal legislation like the Wagner Act went a long way to help workers organize for better wages and working conditions.

Chapter Four

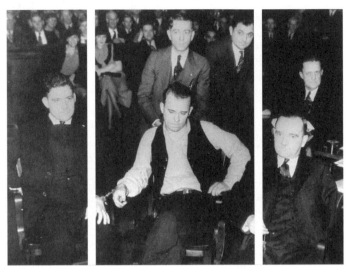

*During the depression, many Americans made heroes of outlaws
who took what they wanted at gunpoint. One desperado, a
brutal thief and a cold-blooded murderer named John Dillinger,
dominated headlines from September 1933 until July 1934,
as he and his violent gang terrorized the Midwest.*

In the News

The early thirties was a time of cynicism and despair, when terrible things happened to good, decent people, when it seemed the poor kept getting poorer while the rich just got richer. The line between good and evil, right and wrong, and even between heroes and villains was no longer clear and clean-cut. It was an era when cops and G-men (FBI agents) were on the take and politicians were crooked, while the biggest gangster in the country was honored for financing soup lines and other acts of charity and bank robbers like John Dillinger were celebrated as Robin Hoods.

Americans in the thirties got hooked on news, and the news gave them a new sense of national solidarity. Coverage of the Capone tax-evasion trial, the Lindbergh kidnapping, and the latest escapades of Bonnie and Clyde gave Americans everywhere a growing sense that crime was a national problem that was getting way out of hand.

Although radio was the hot new medium of the thirties, people did not stop reading newspapers and magazines. Extraordinary events both at home and abroad, such as the implementation of FDR's New Deal, the repeal of Prohibition, labor strikes, crime, the rise of fascism in Europe and Japan, and scientific and aeronautical breakthroughs either directly touched the lives of people or provided a relatively cheap and sensational form of daily entertainment. There were fewer newspapers (the result of numerous mergers) but wider distribution of those that survived. The tabloid style became popular, and the quantity of photographs and comics in newspapers doubled between 1930 and 1940.

Of course, not all stories were gloomy, sensational, or even earth-shaking. Both daily newspapers and weekly magazines like *Reader's Digest, Life,* and *Newsweek* offered a mix of fiction and feature stories to keep adults entertained, while children poured over comic books and newspaper comic strips. Also, crossword puzzles, and

Newspaper Comic Strips

Many of the comic strips popular in the '30s were first established in American newspapers between 1907 and 1920, like "Bringing Up Father," "Gasoline Alley," and "Tillie the Toiler." Some of these strips were fantastic and/or satirical, like Elzie Crisler Segar's "Popeye" and George Herriman's "Krazy Kat," which was aimed more at adults than at children.

During the 1930s the comics page expanded both in quantity of strips and in range of subject matter. Several of the strips, such as Chic Young's domestic comedy "Blondie," have survived for more than sixty years.

A new category emerged in the '30s: the continuous-action adventure strip. This category took many forms: domestic and detective drama, science and space fiction, and, by 1938, war and supermen strips. The earliest adventure strip was "Tarzan," which first appeared in 1929. Its creator, Harold Foster, started a whole new realistic, documentary cartoon style.

Other artists who introduced new cartoon effects were Alex Raymond, first master of the exotic space trip with his strip "Flash Gordon" in 1933, and Milton Caniff, who introduced "Terry and the Pirates" in 1934. Chester Gould's "Dick Tracy," which first appeared in 1931, is considered by many to be the detective strip par excellence, while Al Capp's "Li'l Abner" (first appearance 1934) is considered an excellent example of satirical comic strip art.

No. 1   JUNE, 1938

Superman was created in the early thirties by two Cleveland, Ohio, youths named Joe Shuster and Jerry Siegel. When Action Comics published the first Superman story in 1938, comic book sales exploded.

news about fashion, sports, and hobbies provided fun and diversion from grim depression reality.

Organized Crime Dominates Front-Page News

Some of the most closely followed news stories—and the ones that provided the most lurid headlines—were reports of crime. The all-out war waged between law enforcement and the nation's notorious mobsters and outlaws captivated readers' attention.

Organized crime had come into its own by the 1930s. Organized families of Italian American criminals had taken over control of a large percentage of illegal activities from rival Irish, Jewish, and other gangs in New York, Chicago, and other major cities throughout the country. These various Italian Mafia groups, in turn, fought each other in a bloody nationwide conflict in 1930 and 1931 for control of a nationwide crime network.

In the twenties and early thirties, their most profitable dealings were in the illegal manufacture and sale of bootleg alcohol. After the repeal of Prohibition in 1933, the American Mafia abandoned its bootlegging operations and settled into gambling, labor racketeering, loansharking, narcotics distribution, and prostitution rings. It grew to be the largest and most powerful of U.S. syndicated-crime organizations, often reinvesting its profits in legitimate businesses such as hotels, restaurants, and entertainment ventures. Its first leader was John Torrio, known by some as the "thinking man's criminal."

Prohibition offered Torrio a golden opportunity to put into practice his dream of organizing crime as a business, an approach that eventually influenced gangs all over the country. He also insisted on negotiation instead of violence, an idea that did not become quite as popular. Always eager to avoid strife, Torrio's motto was "There's plenty for everyone."

After he was sent to prison in 1925, Torrio turned over all his holdings to his young right-hand man, Al Capone, who then dominated organized crime in Chicago until 1931. Al "Scarface" Capone soon became one of the most famous gangsters in American history,

Al Capone's (left) friendship with newspaper editor Harry Read convinced Capone that he should behave like the prominent figure he was. "Quit hiding," Read told him. "Be nice to people." Capone became visible at the opera, at sporting events, and charitable functions, including funding soup kitchens like the one below. In an era where most of the adult population drank bootleg alcohol, the bootlegger seemed almost respectable.

turning Chicago into an empire of gambling, prostitution, and bootlegging rackets. His and rival gangs made sensational front-page news prior to the repeal of Prohibition.

In spite of the negative publicity, Capone was not an entirely unsympathetic figure, especially in Chicago. Although he could hardly be considered a Robin Hood, taking from the rich and giving to the poor, Capone did sponsor city soup kitchens and other charitable functions during the de-pression. He was so generous to friends and family that his Christmas shopping alone each year set him back over a hundred thousand dollars. He was known to tip waiters and musicians with hundred-dollar bills and on special occasions handed out diamond belt buckles.

Capone was never convicted for his criminal activities, but in June 1931 the government did indict him for federal income-tax evasion. In October of the same year he was tried,

Capone Meets His Nemesis

Beginning in 1930, after the government had been unable to bring charges against Capone for his mob activities and in the face of increasing pressure from the public to put him behind bars, the U.S. Treasury Department assigned its Special Intelligence Unit to put together a tax-evasion case against Capone. Given the fact that Capone owned no property in his own name and avoided banks, checks, and receipts, the job wasn't going to be easy.

It didn't help that a Treasury agent's salary was typically less than that of a garbage collector, which made mob bribes tempting—that is, until the Untouchables were formed.

The Untouchables were a hand-picked group of federal agents led by a University of Chicago graduate named Eliot Ness. They got their name because, as mob leaders quickly found out, they couldn't be bribed.

At first Ness and his men tried to put a dent in Capone's bootlegging operation in 1930, but their efforts were compared to trying to empty an ocean of beer with a teacup. During the first half of 1930 Ness managed to set the mob's bootlegging operation back about a million dollars—but that was less than 4 percent of what the bootleggers were handing out just in bribes.

It didn't help that by the time Ness swung into action, Capone had already predicted the end of Prohibition and was busy diversifying into other rackets like corrupting labor unions and extorting money from small businesses. Capone personally came to control hundreds of Chicago rackets, including associations for soda pop peddlers, motion picture operators, and Jewish chicken killers.

In 1931 the government hung an eleven-year tax-evasion sentence on Capone.

found guilty, and sentenced to eleven years in prison and $80,000 in fines. He entered the federal penitentiary in Atlanta in May 1932 but was transferred to the new Alcatraz prison in August 1934. (He was eventually paroled and died a slow and painful death of syphilis in Florida in 1947.)

Capone's illegal fortune was enormous. During an era when $50 a week would support a family of six comfortably, a Capone bodyguard made as much as $100 a day. The IRS later estimated Al's 1927 receipts at $100 million, with his personal profit probably approaching $10 million. About 60 percent of the gross came from his bootlegging operations. His largest expense was graft, amounting to $30 million in 1930 alone.

The Rise of the Outlaw

Organized crime was not law enforcement's only headache in the 1930s. Outlaw gangs cropped up that specialized in robbing banks and trains and in kidnapping. The newspapers of the day were always on the lookout for spectacular stories that would distract their readers from the dreary news of the depression, and outlaws made terrific headlines.

In April 1933, an obscure criminal named John Dillinger walked out of an Indiana prison with $5 and a new suit. A year later he was number one on FBI director Hoover's list of public enemies. He was finally gunned down by a squad of G-men outside a Chicago movie theater in July 1934. By then his record included a string of ten murders, four bank robberies, and three jailbreaks.

There were over six thousand gangsters and other interstate evildoers on Hoover's list of public enemies, but outlaws and mob gangsters are two totally different breeds of criminal. Gangsters like Al Capone and Lucky Luciano grew up in urban settings and usually served apprenticeships with youth gangs. Outlaws, on the other hand, were mostly of rural origin and generally came from law-abiding families. While gangsters pursued their ill-gotten gains through ongoing enterprises like bootlegging and narcotics rackets, outlaws specialized in hit-and-run crimes like bank robberies and kidnappings. They dreamed of a heist big enough to retire on, not a successfully organized crime business.

Ma Barker was the matriarch of a gang of outlaw brothers and their friends who engaged in kidnapping, and post office and bank robberies in the twenties and thirties. The "Bloody Barkers" robbed and kidnapped throughout the midwestern United

Gun Molls

A woman who chose to be a gun moll in the 1930s usually linked her fortunes to a male outlaw who made his living by robbing banks, and/or kidnapping people for ransom. Molls were integral to the success of the crimes. They made good money, lived fast lives, and were committed to a code of female honor that penalized "snitches" and "stool pigeons."

Molls were members of three of the most prominent gangs of the '30s: the Dillinger mob of southern Indiana; the Barrow gang (otherwise known as Bonnie and Clyde) of western Texas; and the Barker-Karpis gang of northeastern Oklahoma (led by the mother of several of the gang members, "Ma" Barker).

Federal laws passed in 1934 made aiding and abetting fugitives a felony in itself, so the molls (or mollys as they were sometimes called) had as much to lose as their men. Over twenty women were eventually prosecuted by the federal government for gang-related activity. Although not all fit a single stereotype, molls had a lot in common. A moll was usually young and the child of farming parents or skilled workers. Each had worked at a service job in a hotel or restaurant that had put them in the way of criminals. (Opal Long, for example, fell in with the Dillinger gang while working as a soda fountain attendant in a Chicago hotel.)

Few of the molls ever actually married their outlaw lovers; some were even already married to other men. Yet almost all felt just as bound by love and loyalty to the relationship as if they had been legally married.

States from Minnesota to Texas. All the Barkers met violent deaths.

Clyde Barrow and Bonnie Parker were a small-time but notorious robber team that gained fame through their flamboyant encounters with police. Barrow had been a young outlaw long before meeting Parker in January 1930. After serving twenty months in prison, he teamed up with Bonnie, and they began a twenty-one-month career, often working with other outlaw friends and relatives such as Clyde's brother, Buck Barrow, and Buck's wife, Blanche, Ray Hamilton, and W. D. Jones.

Bonnie and Clyde, as they were popularly known, robbed gas stations, restaurants, and small-town banks, never taking more than $1,500 at a time. Their crime spree spread through Texas, Oklahoma, New Mexico, and Missouri before they were at last betrayed by a friend and gunned down by police in a roadblock ambush.

Murder, Kidnapping and Attempted Assassination

Not all the sensational crime headlines were mob or gang related. Others involved extorting money from the wealthy, starting in March 1932 with a shocking kidnapping

Clyde Barrow, the son of a Texas sharecropper and Bonnie Parker, a waitress from East Dallas joined forces to become two of the most sought after public enemies in the Southwest.

regarded as the world's greatest hero, Charles A. Lindbergh, the young man who had flown the first solo flight across the Atlantic Ocean in 1927. Nicknamed Lucky Lindy and the Lone Eagle, he had almost single-handedly launched the era of transoceanic flight.

Mobbed by admirers and pursued by the press both here and abroad, the Lindberghs built a $50,000, twenty-room stone house at a wooded, secluded spot in central New Jersey. Sometime during the night of Tuesday, March 1, their son was taken from his second-floor nursery by a kidnapper who used a ladder to gain entrance to a window and left no fingerprints but did leave a note demanding $50,000 in ransom, a fortune in depression times. In the days and nights that followed, a desperate Lindbergh sought help from numerous negotiators who claimed to be go-betweens with the kidnapper.

and murder called the "crime of the century." Someone had dared to kidnap and kill the infant son of the man then

Thousands of letters poured into the estate, some expressing sympathy, some with ransom demands or death threats, even some psychic predictions.

Not since Lincoln's assassination had the country been so appalled and so shaken by a crime. President Hoover himself said, "We will move heaven and earth to find out who is the criminal who had the audacity to commit a crime like this."[42]

On May 12, the little boy's remains were discovered by a truck driver; the cause of death was a massive fracture of the skull. It took more than two years of following the trail of passed ransom bills to track down the man accused of the murder, a German-born Bronx carpenter named Bruno Richard Hauptmann. When he was arrested, Hauptmann denied the charge but was found to have over $14,000 of the ransom cash hidden in his garage. It was later discovered that a board cut from his attic floor was used in the ladder. He insisted that he had been home on the night of the kidnapping with his wife, Anna, and that the money was left by Isidor Fisch, a fur dealer he knew who had fled to Germany.

Hauptmann was convicted of the crime and executed. Newspapers ran thousands of articles and photos, often filling several pages with trial coverage. There was even a syndicated comic strip about the crime. Bruno Hauptmann never confessed to the Lindbergh kidnapping,

American aviator Charles Lindbergh made the first solo nonstop flight across the Atlantic Ocean on May 20–21, 1927. When, on March 1, 1932, the Lindberghs' twenty-month-old son was kidnapped, the press sensationalized the tragedy.

A thirty-five-year-old German carpenter named Bruno Hauptmann was charged in September 1934 in connection with the kidnapping and murder of the Lindbergh baby. The renowned journalist H. L. Mencken called the trial "the greatest story since the Resurrection." It was indeed a circus, with hundreds of reporters and spectators swelling the small town to several times its population.

and skepticism and a degree of mystery surrounding the case have persisted for decades.

One of the most shocking crimes of the decade was the attempted assassination of President-elect Roosevelt in Miami in February 1933. He was talking with Chicago mayor Anton Cermak amid a crowd of ten thousand who were welcoming him home from a vacation cruise when six shots rang out. Cermak was struck in the chest and shoulder, a Secret Service agent

was grazed by one of the bullets, and Roosevelt himself doubled up in his seat but called out "I'm all right! I'm all right!" The angry crowd tackled the gunman to the ground. He turned out to be an unemployed bricklayer from New Jersey named Giuseppe Zangara. "I hate all presidents," he told police, "no matter from what country they come."[43] Mayor Cermak was rushed to the hospital, where he died three weeks later of his gunshot wounds. Zangara pleaded guilty to murder and was electrocuted in a Florida state prison two weeks later, on March 20.

Adventure and Disaster in the Skies

In 1932, five years after Lindbergh made his historic flight, Amelia Earhart became the first woman to fly solo across the Atlantic. In January 1935, she became the first person to fly transpacific from Hawaii to California, after ten pilots had lost their lives attempting the same flight. Later that same year, she started to formulate plans for an around-the-world flight. This flight would incorporate two major firsts: she would be the first woman to do it, and she would travel the longest distance possible by circumnavigating the globe at its waist.

In 1932, Amelia Earhart became the first woman to fly solo across the Atlantic. In 1937, Earhart and navigator Fred Noonan disappeared during a trip around the world.

Earhart and her navigator, Fred Noonan, set out in July 1937. Unfortunately, after flying over twenty-two thousand miles, with less than seven thousand miles to go, Earhart's aircraft disappeared. It was determined that the plane went down thirty-five to one hundred miles off the coast of Howland Island. A life raft was on board, but no trace of it has been recovered. President Roosevelt authorized a search using nine naval ships and sixty-six aircraft at an estimated cost of over $4 million. However, on July 18 the search was abandoned.

On May 6, 1937, people who had tuned into a live radio broadcast documenting the arrival of a hydrogen-filled German zeppelin, the *Hindenburg*, at Lakehurst, New Jersey, were horrified as the announcer described the zeppelin crashing into the docking station and exploding.

Heightening International Tensions

Although still preoccupied with life at home, Americans were becoming increasingly aware of world events that could lead to global war. In 1932, newspaper readers learned how Joseph Stalin was terrorizing and starving peasants in the Ukraine. In 1933, Adolf Hitler and his National Socialist (Nazi) Party came to power, proclaiming Germany's new Third Reich, and Japan withdrew from the League of Nations. By July 1936, the news was filled with reports of Japanese forces invading China and of Mussolini pulling Italy out of the League of Nations—more evidence of the international power struggles that were leading inevitably to yet another world war.

In 1939, Germany signed a non aggression pact with the Soviet Union and then invaded neighboring Poland. Britain and France declared war on Germany and the papers became filled with the inescapable horrors of a world at war—as well as all the arguments for and against U.S. participation in it.

Never before had American citizens been so informed about politics and national events or so exposed to human interest stories about everyday men and women like themselves. Advances in media technology had helped make it truly the decade of the common man.

Chapter Five

*Radio became so popular a source of entertainment and news
that it became a serious source of competition for newspapers.*

The Golden Age
of Radio

In 1931, 12 million (40 percent) of the country's 30 million homes owned at least one radio. By 1934, according to *Broadcasting* magazine, that figure jumped to 60 percent, with another 1.5 million installed in cars. By 1939, at least 44 million radios were in use in over 80 percent of homes in the United States. Growth of the radio industry was so dramatic that Congress

passed the Communications Act of 1934 to create the Federal Communications Commission (FCC) to regulate it.

Radio technology in the thirties brought Americans together as never before. For the first time in U.S. history, it was possible to deliver up-to-the-minute news to every household, no matter how rural or remote. This included not just national and international events, but local news, human interest stories, political commentary, and sports events. Radio appealed to every possible human interest, from a morbid fascination with crime and catastrophe to an indulgence in social gossip about movie stars, royalty, and the rich.

Fireside Chats

People also turned to radio for reassurance. FDR used radio to project himself into the living room of every American family so he could explain his policies to them personally and re-

assure them that the country was on its way back to economic sanity.

One of his most appreciated and most persuasive tools was the fireside chat, a periodic radio program carried by NBC in which he personally rallied the country by defining its challenges. Over his almost four complete terms in office, he gave over twenty-eight of these chats. (Not all were officially announced as fireside chats, so the exact count is open to dispute.)

From his first chat on the banking crisis on March 12, 1933, FDR was relaxed, informal, and friendly. He wasted

With his broadcasted fireside chats, FDR had the power to come into living rooms. He shared the country's sorrow, joy, hope, and tragedy.

no time blaming bankers or anyone else, but rather explained exactly why all the banks had been closed and why some of them would not be reopened. He did not sugarcoat the fact that New Deal measures would be drastic and would involve sacrifices. "I do not promise you," he said, "that every bank will be reopened or that individual losses will not be suffered, but there will be no losses that could possibly be avoided. . . . Together we cannot fail."[44]

FDR's use of radio was so impressive that the editor of *Radio Guide* wrote a full-page editorial in the May 26, 1934, issue, praising Roosevelt and praising radio: "Radio has given to the president a weapon such as no ruler has ever known. It enables him instantaneously to answer, overthrow and defeat any false statement concerning himself, his government or his plans. . . . Radio [is] a servant of justice . . . taking knowledge everywhere."[45]

The Fight over News

The public wanted reassurance that the country would make it through the hard times, but they also wanted to know exactly what was really going on. They were hooked on news. Radio brought them stirring news commentators such as Lowell Thomas, Edward R. Murrow, and H. V. Kaltenborn. On

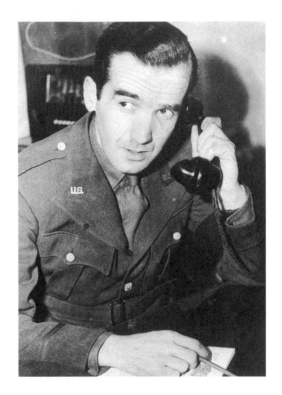

Edward R. Murrow, one of the most famous and respected news broadcasters of all time, was hired by CBS in September 1935.

Friday nights, listeners could tune into "The March of Time," an award-winning news program that re-created and dramatized stories from *Time* magazine. The show's signature line, "time marches on," became a catchphrase of the early '30s. CBS featured a newspaperwoman and magazine writer named Mary Margaret McBride, who hosted a highly respected news talk show, and for listeners who wanted some celebrity news and gossip, Jergens Soap offered "Walter Winchell's Journal," a tell-all gossip show presented in a news format.

Listeners became so dependent on radio for news that after holding a monopoly over news distribution for more than a century, the newspaper industry in the United States suddenly found itself with serious competition. Not surprisingly print journalists spent a good part of the next decade doing everything they could to block the emergence of broadcast journalism.

The *Hindenburg* Disaster

Some of radio's greatest moments occurred as a reporter was commenting live on an actual event and something unexpected happened. One of the more vivid of these memorable events occurred on May 6, 1937, in Lakehurst, New Jersey, where radio reporter Herb Morrison was on hand for the arrival of the huge German zeppelin, the *Graf Hindenburg,* one of Nazi Germany's finest airships.

The airship, which was supposed to represent the greatness of the German Reich and its leader, Adolf Hitler, had made this voyage a number of times before and friends and family of the guest passengers were at Lakehurst waiting for it to moor. Reporter Morrison was there too, thanks to his radio station. The day was rainy and there had been strong thunderstorms earlier. Morrison was recording the event for later rebroadcast. The early part of his recording reflects information about the airship and the day and what was technically necessary to bring the big ship successfully into its mooring.

The zeppelin arrived, but as Morrison started to describe the actual docking process, it suddenly burst into flames.

The Hindenburg *bursts into flames. Coverage of the* Hindenburg *disaster was radio news at its finest. Listeners heard vivid descriptions of the horror of the event as it unfolded, then grieved as they heard reports of searchers retrieving the dead and injured.*

Morrison, in spite of his shock and horror at the terrible tragedy, had the presence of mind to keep talking as the event unfolded. Later, when the story was aired, interviews with survivors were added to Morrison's moving broadcast.

Radio technology did have a tremendous impact on how quickly Americans heard the news. Instead of relying on wire services for news, broadcast networks started hiring their own reporters. In many cases, especially covering political and sports events, they had reporters on hand to describe events as they were happening. Newspapers, in turn, became more competitive by reporting news in more depth. And until the age of television, newspapers still had the advantage of being a visual medium.

In addition to its coverage of news events, radio fostered a national love of sports and pride in sports heroes with its live broadcasts of sports events such as baseball's World Series, and it fed a growing excitement about rapidly advancing technology and breakthroughs in science and medicine. Radio gave people a forum for their political and religious ideas and gave the president a way to reassure a frightened nation. But perhaps most important of all, radio gave depression sufferers the escape of pure entertainment.

Classic Comedy

Radio comedy provided people a much-needed escape from the fear and despair of poverty. It helped them

The Irrepressible Father Coughlin

Another '30s radio personality who quickly learned to manipulate the radio waves for his own power was Father Charles E. Coughlin. The son of a Great Lakes seaman and a seamstress, Coughlin seriously considered entering politics but chose the priesthood instead, and was ordained in Detroit in 1923. He began experimenting with the new medium of radio, broadcasting sermons and talks to children. Soon his sermons started to focus on his political and economic interests, and he began attacking President Hoover. He actively supported FDR in the 1932 elections, but as Coughlin gained more and more listeners nationwide, he moved away from his earlier political views and began expressing reactionary anti-Roosevelt, anti–New Deal sentiments.

To expand on his broadcast politics, Coughlin then started a magazine called *Social Justice*, in which he published shrill attacks on communism, Wall Street, and Jews. The magazine was banned from the mails for violating the Espionage Act and ceased publication in 1942. In the same year the Catholic hierarchy ordered him to stop broadcasting.

Coughlin wrote the books *Christ or the Red Serpent* (1930), *By the Sweat of Thy Brow* (1931), and *The New Deal in Money* (1933). In spite of his critics, he remained pastor in Michigan until his retirement in 1966.

forget what was going on around them for a while and helped them laugh at themselves.

Many of the great stage stars of vaudeville saw the opportunities of radio, but had a hard time making the transition without a live audience to respond to their lines. Gradually, the ones who became successful on radio learned to incorporate recognizable characters and story lines into their stand-up comedy routines. One of the earliest acts to make a hit on radio was a Chicago team who began a series of radio skits for station WGN based on characters they named Sam and Henry. Although actors Charles Correll and Freeman Gosden were white, they based their routines on African American dialects, a popular form of comedic delivery at the time. The show proved so popular that NBC gave the two of them their own national comedy program, renaming the characters Amos and Andy, a show that lasted off and on in radio and TV form until 1954. Amos and Andy ran the Fresh-Air Taxi Company and belonged to the Mystic Knights of the Sea, along with a mutual friend they called the Kingfish. The show was so popular that it spawned toys, candy bars, and a newspaper comic strip. Some of their best remembered expressions are "Buzz me, Miss Blue!" and "Check and double check!"

Other vaudeville comedians started successful radio shows as well, including Ed Wynn, George Jessel, Eddie Cantor, and Fred Allen. Allen (whose face, his wife claimed, was made for radio), premiered in a program called *The Linit Bath Club Revue* in 1930. Allen's sharp wit was not always popular among network executives, however, and only his increasing popularity protected him from constant censorship.

Allen's great radio rival (but personal friend) was Jack Benny, whose own comedy program hit the top ten by the end of 1933. Benny's style was to give the laughs to the other characters on his show and react to their humorous situations, making himself look like the fool. Almost immediately, Benny began a long-running "feud" with Allen that many listeners feel climaxed in the famous "King for a Day" skit when Benny supposedly stripped to his briefs in one of the wildest shows ever aired. Over the years, both Allen and Benny added other radio actors to portray regular characters in their skits, but unlike Allen, Benny later successfully continued his career in film and television.

A vaudeville husband-and-wife team destined for radio, film, and television stardom was George Burns and Gracie Allen. Burns met Gracie in 1922 and established a vaudeville act with Gracie playing a scatterbrained blonde straight man. Several years

Amos 'n' Andy *(above) was one of the most beloved and popular radio programs in the history of radio. At its peak, it is said cities literally came to a halt while the show was being broadcast. Everyone wanted to hear their favorite two characters and their daily misfortunes. The series remained on the air for nearly thirty years. (Right) Jack Benny starred in his own radio show in 1932, and became an immediate hit. Among the many running gags on his show were his stinginess, his ancient Maxwell automobile, and the vault in his basement where he kept his money. His favorite phrases were "Now cut that out!" and "Wait a minute. Wait a Minute! WAIT A MINUTE!"*

later, they realized that it was Gracie who got most of the laughs, so they reversed the concept. Gracie contin-

ued to develop the dizzy dame character while George took on the straight role:

GEORGE: What's that?

GRACIE: Electric cords. I had them shortened. This one's for the iron, this one's for the floor lamp.

GEORGE: Why did you shorten them?

GRACIE: To save electricity.

. . . . .

GEORGE: Gracie, what do you think of television?

GRACIE: I think it's wonderful—I hardly ever watch radio anymore.[46]

Another vaudeville couple who made it big on radio was Jim and Marian Jordan who starred in a program sponsored by Johnson's Wax called *Fibber McGee and Molly*, a couple who lived at 79 Wistful Vista. Fibber was a braggart who could never seem to finish anything he started, and always seemed to become involved in ill-fated crusades and schemes. Molly, the antithesis to Fibber, was patient, kind, and level-headed, and was the only

Starting in September 1930, comedy team George Burns and Gracie Allen had their own show on CBS called Isn't It Fun. *Burns has said, "I was nothing until I was 27 years old. Then I met Gracie—the best break I ever had in my life."*

person who could keep Fibber in check. Listeners loved the regular characters who appeared in Fibber and Molly's lives: rival and pal Throckmorton P. Gildersleeve (who was always threatening to clean Fibber's clock); Abigail Uppington, the snooty society matron; Mayor LaTrivia, whom Fibber always managed to unravel; and Doc Gamble, the "bone bender." Also in this mob were the joke-telling Old Timer ("That's pretty good, Johnny, but that ain't the way I heerd it!"); Nick Depopulous, who ran the Greek restaurant; and Wallace Wimpole, with a droopy-dog voice and a big wife named Sweetie Face.

Radio comedy had some pretty unusual acts, but none was stranger than Edgar Bergen's. Bergen was a ventriloquist with a wooden dummy named Charlie McCarthy. In spite of the fact that listeners couldn't see the act, it became an instant hit. In the minds and ears of the listeners, Charlie was real and came up with some great sayings, such as "Ambition is just an excuse for those without the good sense to be lazy" and "Hard work never killed anyone, but why take the chance?"[47] This program was also known as *The Chase and Sanborn Hour*, a reference to the show's long-standing sponsor, Chase and Sanborn coffee.

Drama and Detective Stories

Radio listeners of the 1930s loved private eyes, continuing the love affair Americans had started with pulp crime magazines such as *True Detective* in the twenties. One of the earliest detective dramas, sponsored by the National Surety Company, featured one of its operators, Detective Harkness. Based on the company's real case files and solved by the fictitious Harkness, the stories were presented as first-person narratives. The show opened with an announcement by Harkness: "I'm not going to waste any time or words getting into tonight's story. One day, not so long ago, I entered my office in the National Surety Company's building as the phone was ringing."[48] Harkness went on to tell the story as though he were reading it from his own file. Two other radio crime series that successfully used the first-person narrative style were *Sam Spade* and *Yours Truly, Johnny Dollar*. The technique allowed the listener to relate immediately to the main character and pulled the audience directly into the story.

Most radio detectives were the hard-boiled type originally found in the pages of the dime novels or pulp magazines and later more finely honed by writers such as James M. Cain, Dashiell Hammett, and Raymond Chandler. These private detectives

Sam Spade

The character of one of this country's most-read detective novelists, Dashiell Hammett's Sam Spade, came alive for radio listeners in *The Adventures of Sam Spade* starring Howard Duff. Spade was the classic '30s detective: ruthless, morally ambiguous, but not without scruples. Sam Spade could not be bribed even though he appeared to be low enough to accept a bribe. However, he was not opposed to the occasional bonus of dubious legality. In *The Maltese Falcon,* he turns the woman he loves, Brigid O'Shaughnessy, over to the police when he finds out that she was the one responsible for the death of Spade's detective partner.

The Sam Spade of radio could be brutal as well as lovable, as reflected in the eyes of his secretary, Effie. Duff played the character tongue-in-cheek while maintaining an aspect of the grittiness of the novels. Compare Duff's Spade to that played by Humphrey Bogart, which is probably closer to the Hammett creation and is usually considered the definitive Sam Spade. Bogart appeared on radio in Academy Award Theater's version of *The Maltese Falcon.*

Radio also produced another sort of detective character, one with more intellectual deductive powers and less brute force. One of the earliest was the famous Charlie Chan. In *The Adventures of Charlie Chan,* Detective Chan (portrayed by Ed Begley) used his brain to solve the crime and did so with style and humor. The formula was pretty much the same from week to week: Charlie Chan of the Honolulu Police Force, crack detective and worldwide celebrity, happened upon a good case of murder in an interesting or exotic locale, usually not Honolulu but San Francisco. One or two of Charlie's sons (usually identified chronologically as number one son and number two son, detective wanna-be's themselves), offered "Pop" their assistance and then proceeded to spend the rest of the film getting in the way, providing comic relief, until Charlie solved the case in spite of them. Along the way, Detective Chan could be counted on for numerous pithy Chinese proverbs (some pithier than others) such as: "Necessity mother of invention, but sometimes stepmother of deception" and "Truth like oil—will in time rise to the surface." Referring to one of his interfering sons, Chan said, "Sometimes

tended to operate by their own rough code of justice, often outside of the law, to apprehend society's criminals. They lived and worked on the seamier side of the big city, where the rich got richer and the poor got poorer and life was seldom fair.

quickest way to brain of young sprout is by impression on other end."[49]

A more serious radio detective, based on a famous fictional character created by Sir Arthur Conan Doyle, Sherlock Holmes, was played over the years by a number of excellent actors including Basil Rathbone. He, too, was known for his deductive reasoning and pithy statements to his cohort Dr. Watson: "How often have I said to you that when you have eliminated the impossible, whatever remains, however improbable, must be the truth?"[50]

Some heroic opponents of crime were undercover detectives, like pilot Captain Midnight. In the beginning, Captain Midnight was simply an undercover name for Jim "Red" Albright, who regularly piloted cargo and passengers while secretly trying to gather information on a gang of criminals. However, by the end of the show's first season, Captain Midnight became a larger-than-life cult hero only known by that name. Captain Midnight was constantly trying to stop the plans of the evil Ivan Shark and his daughter Fury. Shark remained as Midnight's evil nemesis throughout the heyday of radio. Captain Midnight was aided in his efforts by Chuck Ramsey and Patsy Donovan, members of his Secret Squadron, and Ichabod Mudd, Midnight's mechanic. The show was especially appealing to younger listeners who were invited to become active members in Captain Midnight's Secret Squadron by sending in for badges and decoder rings. Eventually, the series moved from radio to film and finally to television.

Science Fiction and Adventure

Perhaps nothing provided an escape from reality as dramatically as radio science fiction. Here, too, radio took its cue from the pulps, with stories taken from magazines like *Air Wonder* and *Amazing Stories.*

One of the first science fiction radio series was *Buck Rogers in the Twenty-Fifth Century,* in which a person from the thirties found himself in the twenty-fifth century, where, despite some very determined enemies, life could be wonderful. Buck's sidekicks were the beautiful and strong-willed Wilma Darling and the brilliant scientist Dr. Huer, who was constantly inventing amazing and handy machines. Society's enemies were usually ruthless, exotic, and out to destroy the universe, but with Wilma and Dr. Huer's help, Buck somehow always prevailed.

Another science fiction radio series during this period was *Flash Gordon.* Like *Buck Rogers,* the radio series was aimed at the juvenile audience. The plots were black-and-white and almost cartoonish in their dramatizations.

The War of the Worlds

On Halloween 1938, Orson Welles's Mercury Theater produced a play called *Invasion from Mars* that some thought bordered more on horror than escapist science fiction. (Welles also wrote and narrated the play.) Welles played a frightened and horrified news announcer describing the landing and subsequent killing spree of a spaceship filled with Martians. He was so convincing—and there were no disclaimers before the program started explaining that it was just a play—that many people thought the program was an actual news broadcast and panicked. Thousands of supposedly rational adults called the radio station for more news; thousands more ran out of their homes and into the streets, screaming in panic.

Welles's production was actually a metaphor about the real world, a sort of reflection on what was occurring in Europe at the time told in future tense. By taking something fantastic and placing it into a world already on edge from de-

The radio programs Orson Welles recorded in the late thirties and early forties transformed radio forever.

pression and fear of war, Welles conjured even more horrific images in the minds of his listeners.

Unlike his counterpart, Buck Rogers, Flash Gordon was born into a futuristic society in a different universe. When the planet Mongo threatens to destroy the earth, Flash and his girlfriend Dale Arden hop a spaceship and set out to save it.

Action and adventure stories like *The Lone Ranger* were also immensely popular with kids in the 1930s. There probably wasn't a kid in America who didn't recognize the Lone Ranger's theme song (actually Rossini's *William Tell Overture*) or slogan: "A fiery horse with a speed of light, a cloud of dust, and a hearty 'Hi-Yo, Silver!'"[51] "Hi-yo Silver, Away!" became a familiar playground exclamation.

The Lone Ranger is a young man named John Reid, the sole survivor of a group of Texas Rangers who were ambushed by outlaws. (His brother

Daniel was one of the victims.) An Indian named Tonto finds him and nurses him back to health. When he recovers, Reid dons a black mask made from his dead brother's vest, mounts his stallion, Silver, and from then on roams the West as the Lone Ranger to aid those in need, with Tonto's help, and to fight evil and establish justice wherever he goes.

Soap Opera

A favorite daytime radio program of housewives (and many unemployed men) was the soap opera. Soap operas were dramatic serial programs that got their name because most of the major sponsors were manufacturers of soap and detergents. In fact, the plots and dialogues of the original radio soap operas (such as *Oxydol's Own Ma Perkins*, the first successful soap, which premiered in Chicago in 1933) were actually nothing more than fifteen-minute skits centered around women using soap. A year later, Proctor and Gamble, another major soap manufacturer, hired a writer named Irna Phillips to create an ongoing serial about the lives of a family of established characters. Three of the shows she subsequently created, *The Guiding Light, Days of Our Lives,* and *As the World Turns,* proved so popular that they made the transition to TV in the 1950s (expanded into a thirty-

minute format) and are still running today. Other popular soap operas of the thirties were *The Romance of Helen Trent* and *Jack Armstrong, All-American Boy* (the story of a clean-cut high school athlete and his friends).

The classic American soap opera was a continuing play about a middle-class family living in a small town. The dialogue was usually melodramatic and the plots were complicated by incredible twists and turns of sin and violence over the years. In a typical episode, the son of a small-town lawyer confronted his father's first wife's second husband for having an affair with his (the son's) pretty young wife, who everyone thought was killed in a train crash two years ago but who had actually started a new life as an exotic dancer in a nearby town after only suffering temporary amnesia from a blow to the head during the crash.

Not all soap operas were sponsored by soap companies, however. *Just Plain Bill* was created by General Mills to promote its Wheaties, Breakfast of Champions cereal. The series (which started in 1933 and ran for twenty years) was the story of a barber in the small town of Hartville.

Music

For many young people, swing music was the attraction of radio, a style of jazz that catapulted band leaders such as Benny Goodman, Harry James, Tommy and Jimmy Dorsey, and Glenn Miller into '30s stardom. A number of jazz soloists also became popular in the '30s, such as pianist Fats Waller and tenor saxophonist Ornette Coleman. Also considered great were saxophonists Lester Young, Johnny Hodges, and Willie Smith; trumpeters Roy Eldridge, Buck Clayton, and Cootie Williams; trombonists Jack Teagarden and Dickie Wells; and blues singers Bessie Smith and Billie Holiday.

Not everyone had the opportunity (or money) to catch these musicians live, but all one had to do was turn on the radio for an instant party. One of the hottest dance crazes of the '30s was the jitterbug (also known as jump), a sort of wild, aerobic dance with couples doing a lot of swinging and lifting while holding one or both of each other's hands. There were a number of different versions of jitterbug. One was the Lindy hop (named for Charles Lindbergh's transatlantic flight), in which dancers usually did two slow "dig" steps (ball of the foot, then the

By 1936, the Big Band craze had exploded with a number of popular orchestras. Band directors such as Benny Goodman (pictured) and Count Basie were incredibly popular, and by World War II, Duke Ellington had mastered swing and brought it to its highest pinnacle.

heel) and two quicksteps (one foot back, one in place). Another was the jive, in which dancers took a step to each side and then executed two "shuffles" (side step, almost close other foot, side step).

A newspaper poll held in late 1931 showed that Guy Lombardo and Paul Whiteman led the most popular dance orchestras, while winners in the vocalist category included Rudy Vallee, Kate Smith, and a new singer who had made his debut over CBS in September of that year, Bing Crosby. One of the most popular male vocalists was a comedian with his own radio show named Eddie Cantor.

If you listened to music on the radio in 1934, you could open up your latest issue of *Popular Songs* magazine to learn the words to your favorite songs. That year, some of the hits included "I Get a Kick out of You," "Blue Moon," "I Only Have Eyes for You," and "Santa Claus Is Coming to Town." Even composer George Gershwin had his own radio show, starting in February on WJZ/NBC and called *Music by Gershwin* (Feenamint was the sponsor).

Country music gained national popularity on radio, too, with a program broadcast out of Nashville, Tennessee, called *Grand Ole Opry*. Founded by George Dewey Hay, who had helped organize a similar program out of Chicago called the *National Barn Dance*, the show flourished through the heyday of radio and on into the television era.

The music of the Opry developed from Uncle Dave Macon's ballads of rural laborers in the 1920s, through the string bands, cowboy music, and western swing of the 1930s, and back to the traditional music characterized by the career of Roy Acuff, who was propelled into stardom by the Opry in the late 1930s. Acuff, a vocalist, songwriter, and fiddle player, became the "King of Country Music" in the mid-1930s with the mournful musical traditions of southeastern rural whites.

Radio in the 1930s truly added richness to American life. It provided news, entertainment, sports, religion, politics, culture, and education. Radio was a terrific marketing tool, and a powerful medium for politicians. Comedy and drama knit families closer together, while the president's fireside chats brought the nation itself closer together in a time of fear and terrible depression. Not until television came into its own after World War II did a twentieth century invention give so much to the American people.

Chapter Six

New Yorkers discovered the beaches of Coney Island after the subway was completed in the late 1920s. In the thirties, the resort became known as the "nickel empire" because five cents could buy any one of a number of incredible diversions including fast food, roller coaster rides, carnival games, and freak shows featuring such attractions as Singing Lotto, Fat Girl, and Spider Boy.

Having Fun in the Thirties

Life during the Great Depression of the 1930s was not all austerity and gloom. A remarkable number of inexpensive diversions besides radio provided Americans with a temporary escape from personal problems, not to mention anxiety over the national economy and worsening international political crises. Because of the New Deal, Americans had incredible op-portunities to soak up free culture. Wherever you lived, you could watch or participate in sports, play games, attend free or cheap plays, concerts, and art exhibits, learn a hobby, or pic-nic in the park.

Motion Pictures

The most popular of these escapes by far was the magic of motion pictures.

During the decade, movie studios produced more than five thousand feature-length films. Americans flocked to theaters to see them, despite their poverty and unemployment, purchasing tickets at a rate of 60 to 80 million a week. For about a quarter, a person could buy a couple of hours of escape from the drabness and monotony of everyday life and be caught up in glamour, adventure, excitement, and romance. Movie stars became popular idols. Sexy Jean Harlow's platinum-blonde hair sent thousands of girls into bathrooms experimenting with peroxide bleach. When heartthrob Clark Gable took off his shirt in the romantic comedy *It Happened One Night* and revealed that he wasn't wearing an undershirt, men's underwear sales actually went into a slump.

Clark Gable, known as the "King of Hollywood," was an extremely popular film star for thirty years. Audiences found his rugged masculinity and "I'm just a regular kinda guy" attitude appealing.

Technological innovations such as sound and color created a revolution in scriptwriting and directing. Audiences wanted action—but they also wanted believable dialogue and coherent story lines, lavish sets, extravagant dance numbers, and sophisticated special effects. The movie studios gave them all that and more.

The American film industry was dominated by five major corporate-style studios in the 1930s: Twentieth Century Fox (formed in 1935 from the merger of Twentieth Century Pictures and the Fox Film Corporation), Metro-Goldwyn-Mayer (MGM), Paramount, Warner Brothers, and RKO. Two other minor studios were close behind: Columbia and Universal. MGM was the biggest and most star-studded of them all. MGM had the largest "stable" of stars under contract, including Joan Crawford, Clark Gable, Myrna Loy, William Powell, Norma Shearer, Jean Harlow, Robert Montgomery, and Spencer Tracy. MGM stars Clark Gable and Joan Crawford were called the king and queen of Hollywood. Paramount Studios was a close

Luring Audiences into Movie Houses

Although Americans went to the movies in droves each week, theater owners found they had to be competitive if they wanted to attract large enough audiences to stay in business. At first, they offered special "double features" and games after the movie presentation in which participants could win cash prizes. Some offered amateur talent competitions. Giveaways such as cheap radios became a popular incentive. On certain particularly slow nights each week, women were given individual pieces of china or silverware so that if they went to the movies on a steady basis, they could accumulate complete sets.

In 1932 a Colorado theater manager named Charles Yeager invented a craze called bank nights. By 1936, over a third of the country's theaters had adopted it. The way it worked was simple. Theater patrons wrote their names in a large book in the lobby. Numbers next to their names coincided with the numbers on special tickets kept in the box office. On bank night (usually a slow Monday or Tuesday), a winning ticket was picked out of a drum onstage by a child picked at random and the winner, if he or she was lucky enough to be in the audience that night, had three minutes to get onstage to claim the prize. The prize usually started out at $150 but was increased each week if the winner didn't appear. By the end of 1937, the more than five thousand theaters participating in bank night were distributing almost $1 million a week in prizes. The Saturday Evening Post reported that "it's got to the point where nobody can schedule a basketball game, a church sociable or a bridge party on Tuesday night because everyone's at the local theaters hoping to cash in on Bank Night." In some places, like Des Moines, Iowa, the crowds got so large sometimes that the police and fire departments had to be called out to control them. Even the taverns complained because beer sales were down on bank nights.

Shirley Temple

Much to the financial delight of Twentieth Century Fox, audiences loved their pint-size star Shirley Temple, radiating optimism and singing and dancing in hits like *Stand Up and Cheer* (1934), *Bright Eyes* (1934), *Heidi* (1937), *Rebecca of Sunnybrook Farm* (1938), and *The Little Princess* (1939). From 1935 to 1938, Shirley was the number-one box-office attraction in the world, outdoing even Gable, Will Rogers, and the dancing team of Astaire and Rogers. Another child star, Deanna Durbin, was a little older but had a terrific voice. Sonja Henie, older still, was known for her skating as well as acting talents. British producers came up with their own child star, a three-year-old named Binkie Stewart, but in spite of her nine films and cute dimples, she never became the hit Shirley was. Shirley's box-office success was eventually overtaken in 1939 by another young star, MGM's Mickey Rooney.

Known for her blonde ringlets, appealing lisp, and ability to sing and tap-dance, Shirley Temple became a celebrity in 1934 when she starred in five films, including Now and Forever, Little Miss Marker, *and* Bright Eyes. *At the end of that year she was given a special Academy Award.*

second, boasting stars such as Marlene Dietrich, Gary Cooper, Fredric March, Maurice Chevalier, and Claudette Colbert.

The 1930s began with a number of film firsts. Silent star Greta Garbo, now nicknamed "the divine Garbo," spoke her first immortal, husky Swedish-accented words in the film *Anna Christie* in 1930. ("Gimme a viskey, ginger ale on the side, and don't be stingy, baby.") A young blonde star named Jean Harlow appeared in her first major role in Howard Hughes's World War I aviation epic, *Hell's Angels*, in 1930, the same year the first of Hollywood's dramatic prison pictures was produced by MGM—*The Big House* starring Wallace Beery in one of his most hard-boiled roles. It was also the year John Wayne made his debut in his first major role, a western titled *The Big Trail*.

Adventure lovers couldn't seem to get enough of Tarzan movies. The well-muscled Olympic swimming star Johnny Weismuller portrayed a vine-swinging, jungle-calling ape man in 1932 in the first of his twelve films as "lord of the jungle" in *Tarzan the Ape Man*. (In the first six of these films, his companion Jane was played by costar

Maureen O'Sullivan.) Other wide-screen adventures included *The Adventures of Robin Hood* (1938), starring Errol Flynn as Robin Hood and Olivia de Havilland as Maid Marian, the costliest film ever made by Warner

Until Jean Harlow appeared on screen, the vamp usually had dark hair, while the "good" girl was blonde. But Jean's platinum-blonde hair was so unique, and her gowns so low-cut, that the expression "blonde bombshell" was coined to describe her.

Brothers up to that time. Universal's *Flash Gordon*, a series starring Buster Crabbe, premiered in 1936.

One of the most extravagant—and expensive—films of the thirties starred Claudette Colbert in Cecil B. DeMille's opulent production of *Cleopatra* (1934). Another expensive film was the disaster movie *San Francisco* (1936), known for its spectacular twenty-minute earthquake sequence; the picture was MGM's greatest financial success until *Gone with the Wind* three years later.

Warner Brothers developed its own style by producing tough, realistic gangster movies in the thirties, including *Little Caesar* (1930) with Edward G. Robinson as snarling mobster Enrico Bandello, who meets his inevitable fate with the words, "Mother of mercy, is this the end of Rico?", *The Public Enemy* (1931) starring a swaggering, cocky urban gangster portrayed by James Cagney, and Howard Hughes's hard-hitting gangster film *Scarface* (1932), directed by Howard Hawks.

Gone with the Wind

Independent producer David O. Selznick served as a one-man film industry, with tremendous authority and power over the selection of stars and decisions of directors. *Gone with the Wind* (1939) was his biggest triumph. He purchased film rights to the novel from author Margaret Mitchell for $50,000, cast the stars for the film (gambling on a young, unknown actress named Vivien Leigh as Scarlett O'Hara), fought with and bullied director George Cukor and finally dismissed him, and insisted on using the audacious words of Rhett Butler's farewell ("Frankly, my dear, I don't give a damn") in defiance of the Hays Office. He was fined $5,000 for using the word "damn." Although he had originally intended to make the film his own independent production, the fact that highly paid contract superstar Clark Gable was borrowed from MGM and the subsequent high price of the film forced Selznick to agree to let MGM release the film (and receive half the profits).

Scarface was required by the newly formed Hays office, which set production codes for the depiction of sex and violence on film, to add the qualifying subtitle *The Shame of the Nation* to its main title to keep from sounding as though the movie was glorifying gangsters. *I Am a Fugitive from a Chain Gang* (1932), an uncompromising "serious" film, dealt with such subjects as chain gangs and prison reform and promoted the social reform of a corrupt court system.

Universal had great success with horror movies such as its 1931 version of *Dracula* directed by Tod Browning and starring Bela Lugosi as the vampire. Its next feature was James Whale's gothic *Frankenstein* (1931) with an unbilled Boris Karloff as the hulking, malevolent zombie. One of the earliest uses of special effects animation was in RKO's spectacular, campy adventure/fantasy film *King Kong* (1933), starring Fay Wray as the attractive object of the giant ape's desire, held in his clutching hands just before he meets his spectacular death on top of New York's Empire State Building. Other classic horror films of the '30s include Bela Lugosi and Boris Karloff in *The Black* *Cat* (1934), *The Old Dark House* (1932), *Dr. Jekyll and Mr. Hyde* (1932), *The Invisible Man* (1933), and the *Bride of Frankenstein* (1935).

And then there were musicals. Busby Berkeley created dazzling precision dance patterns in extravagant musicals with silly plots and lavish sets such as *42nd Street* and *Gold Diggers of 1933*. Other popular musicals starred

Busby Berkeley, director of the 1935 film Gold Diggers of 1935, *taught the camera to dance with eye-popping overhead shots of chorus girls in kaleidoscopic poses at a time when most musical numbers were filmed straight-on, as if the film audience were watching a musical on stage.*

Ginger Rogers and Fred Astaire dancing their hearts out in *The Gay Divorcee* (1934), *Top Hat* (1935), *Swing Time* (1936), and *Follow the Fleet* (1936). Mickey Rooney was such a popular star of musicals that he did sixteen of them over a space of two decades. The fourth (and one of the most popular) of the Andy Hardy series was *Love Finds Andy Hardy* (1938), in which Rooney stars with young teenage costars Lana Turner and Judy Garland.

In the field of comedy, the old pie-in-the-face vaudeville routines were elevated to new heights of looniness with the Marx Brothers in classic comedies like *A Night at the Opera*, made in 1935. Groucho played the wise-cracking mastermind of their screwball plots, while Chico was the fast-talking schemer, and Harpo the lecherous half-wit whose clowning always got everyone else into trouble. Other madcap Marx Brothers movies included *Animal Crackers* (1930), *Horse Feathers* (1932), and *Duck Soup* (1933).

Cartoons and Newsreels

The advancements in movie color and sound inspired cartoon shorts and films as well. The master of full-length feature cartoon films was Walt Disney. Songs from Disney movies like "Who's Afraid of the Big Bad Wolf?" and "Heigh-ho, Heigh-ho, It's Off to Work

We Go" were widely sung by kids and adults alike. Disney characters such as Mickey Mouse, Donald Duck, and the dwarf Dopey all spawned popular books and toys. Cartoon shorts were produced to show in theaters before the main feature, and by 1932, there were already over a million boys and girls belonging to Mickey Mouse clubs all over the United States, cosponsored by theater managers and local businessmen to stimulate matinee attendance and to "teach good citizenship."

Another major development in the film industry in the 1930s that became an instant hit was the introduction of newsreels, beginning with the *March of Time* in 1934. Although they could not be as current as newspapers or radio, they offered the visual appeal that radio lacked and that newspapers could only approximate with still photographs. As America approached the end of the decade and the increasing probability of involvement in the escalating world aggression, newsreels provided graphic images of world events and figures that could not help but influence American patriotism.

Fads and Crazes

Roller skating and bicycling, especially among adults, also became popular. Manufacturers competed to turn out affordable models, but those who couldn't buy could always find some-place to rent. With kids, the mania for wheels included "soap box" derbies in which they raced homemade cars constructed out of scraps of wood, old boxes and found wheels.

Soap Box Derbies

Since the Soap Box Derby got its start in the depths of the Great Depression, the story of Robert's racer, and its disappointing round trip to Ohio, has been repeated thousands of times. In 1933 a photographer named Myron Scott was photographing three boys, each sitting in a cratelike frame fixed to baby-buggy wheels, rolling down a bumpy hill in Dayton. Scott invited the boys to come back a week later and bring their friends for a bigger race. Nineteen racers came. A considerable crowd gathered. One of the contestants was a local twelve-year-old named Bob Gravett, who had painted the number 7 on his car; it was the easiest number to draw, he explained. An image of Old No. 7 has been used ever since on the official Soap Box Derby logo.

The first All-American Soap Box Derby race was held in Dayton, Ohio, in 1934. The following year, the WPA built a permanent track site for the youth racing classic, Derby Downs.

By late summer of 1933 Scott's races were drawing hundreds of cars and their young drivers and up to forty-thousand spectators. The official Soap Box Derby began the next year in Dayton with thirty-four winners of local races from all over the Midwest pitted against one another. In 1935 the competition moved to Akron because the publisher of the *Akron Beacon-Journal* promised the Derby's first sponsor, Chevrolet, that it would build a permanent track. Scott's creation was a peculiarly American institution. Part spinoff from automobile racing and part spinoff from downhill sledding on Flexible Flyers, it thrived on the passion of teenage boys for anything that has four wheels and flies, if only down a hill under the power of gravitational pull.

The racers soon moved beyond orange crates and the rickety wooden soap boxes that gave the race its name. The winning racer in 1934, steered by Bob Turner of Muncie, Indiana, was built from laminated wood taken from a saloon bar.

Endurance competitions like flagpole sitting were very popular in the thirties. Either to win a bet or to invite the nickel-and-dime contributions of onlookers and supporters, sitters expanded their efforts to include other feats. Young people sat in trees for days and nights on end to set records, make some money, and gain publicity for themselves. Some were injured in falls; a number were even struck by lightning, but that didn't seem to slow down the fad. Some people engaged in eating marathons of clams, raw eggs, spaghetti, hot dogs, whatever was available. Bicycling, walking, radio listening, doughnut eating, roller skating, and even kissing marathons were also common. One of the most depressing was the dance marathon, where crowds of people seemed to be morbidly drawn to watching exhausted

Some people escaped the depression by escaping into a world of fabulous art, bumpers, flashing lights, bells, flippers, and racing steel balls. Pinball, a fast-paced game of skill and luck, was invented in 1931 and became an instant sensation.

couples drag each other across the dance floor days at a time in hopes of winning a much-needed cash prize.

Parlor and card games like bridge were immensely popular among adults. By 1932, books on bridge instruction were making national best-seller lists and it was estimated that over 20 million Americans were playing bridge. Bingo (or its cousins beano or keno) became popular not just at church socials but when entertaining at home. In 1931 an unemployed Philadelphia engineer named Charles B. Darrow invented a board game he called Monopoly. He got Parker Brothers to manufacture it in 1935 and it took the nation by storm that Christmas season. People found it very satisfying to get rich quickly by playing with scrip money and investing it in make-believe real-estate deals.

Miniature golf was another hot fad of the thirties. Almost any good-sized vacant lot was adequate for a miniature golf course, and the course itself could be constructed in about a week at a cost of roughly $2,000. In 1930 alone, it was estimated that $150 million was invested in courses and another $225 million was being spent annually by players. Unfortunately, this fad flashed brightly for a year or so and then burnt itself out, leaving most of the courses to turn back into weedy, vacant lots in a year or two.

Sports in the Thirties

Depression pocketbooks cut into sports attendance as a whole, but some sports, like college football, were actually up from the 1920s. College football became so popular that by 1938 some people began complaining that there were too many postseason bowl games. Originally the Rose Bowl stood alone, but in 1935 the Orange Bowl was added, in 1936 the Sun Bowl, and in 1937 both the Sugar Bowl and the Cotton Bowl. (Two other '30s additions, the Eastern Bowl and the Coal Bowl, didn't last long.) Two notable college football awards were created in the early thirties: the Knute Rockne Trophy, awarded to the national champion at the end of the season, and the Heisman Trophy for outstanding player of the year. The first Heisman Trophy was awarded in 1935 to Jay Berwanger, star runner, passer, kicker, and defensive player for the University of Chicago. That year the Rockne Trophy went to Southern Methodist University.

Americans avidly followed international Olympics competitions, especially in 1932 when both the summer and winter games were held in the United States (the summer games at Los Angeles and the winter games at Lake Placid, New York). An average of over sixty thousand spectators a day attended the games, far exceeding the attendance of any previously held Olympics. The most well known performance of any Olympian athlete in the 1930s, however, took place not in the United States but in Berlin, Germany, in 1936 when African American Jesse Owens scored stunning victories in a number of running and jumping events. He and several other African Americans not only won gold for the United States, but shattered the myth of Aryan superiority that Adolf Hitler had wanted the Olympics to further.

Fine Arts and the WPA

Americans in the thirties did not just escape into the fun of sports and popular culture such as movies and radio. Because of the New Deal, they also had the unprecedented opportunity to

In 1938, fullback Dave Anderson (above) helped the California Bears win a 13-0 victory over Alabama in the Rose Bowl. Called "Andy" or "The Swede," Anderson played in the leather helmet era with no face mask. Starters played both offense and defense, and it was common for regulars to play the entire game. (Right) On August 1,1936, at the Berlin Olympics, Jesse Owens won four gold medals, proving wrong Adolf Hitler's pronouncement that the Aryans would win over Jews and blacks.

soak up cheap or free culture. The New Deal's WPA (Works Progress Administration) did more than put shovels in workers' hands and construct buildings. It sponsored musicians, actors, and artists to provide free or cheap concerts, plays, art exhibits, and even self-improvement courses like music and craft lessons. It hired playwrights, directors, scene designers, actors, make-up artists, and musicians who otherwise would have remained on breadlines. The WPA also provided free or inexpensive puppet shows, dance recitals, musical presentations, and dramas. Never before or since has our government so extensively sponsored the arts.

The New Deal arts projects provided work for jobless artists, but they also had a larger mission: to promote American art and culture and to give more Americans access to what Roosevelt described as "an abundant life." The projects saved thousands of artists from poverty and despair and enabled Americans all across the country to see an original painting for

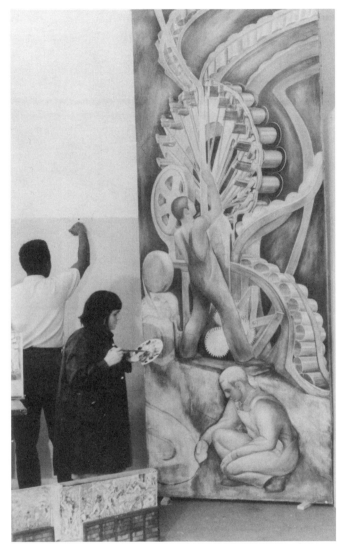

The WPA provided work for painters and sculptors with federal projects such as the Federal Art Gallery in New York City (1939).

the first time, attend their first professional live theater, or take their first music or drawing class.

The first of the U.S. federal art programs was the Public Works Art Project (PWAP). It was organized in December 1933 with funds from the Civil Works Administration to find meaningful work for unemployed artists. It was directed by the financier and painter Edward Bruce, who gave the project its focus, advising the artists it hired to use the "American scene" as their subject matter.

The PWAP initiated over 700 mural projects, 7,000 easel paintings and watercolors, about 750 sculptures, and more than 2,500 works of graphic art, to embellish nonfederal public buildings and parks.

Some of the more famous works produced through the PWAP were the collaborative murals painted in the Coit Memorial Tower at San Francisco, Grant Wood's mural for Iowa State College at Ames; Ben Shahn's mural designs on the theme of Prohibition; and Paul Cadmus's "The Fleet's In," which triggered a national controversy at the PWAP's 1934 national exhibition at the Corcoran Gallery of Art, Washington, D.C., when the U.S. Navy insisted it be removed because it depicted sailors carousing on shore leave.

The PWAP ended in June 1934, after having employed 3,749 artists at an expenditure of $1,312,177. Many of the projects that were left incomplete at this time, especially murals in the design stage, were continued through the summer of 1935 under state programs funded by the Federal Emergency Relief Administration, and some were finally finished in the early months of the Works Progress (later Projects) Administration's Federal Art Project.

The WPA Federal Writers' Project

The Federal Writers' Project was a program established in the United States in 1935 by the WPA to provide jobs for unemployed writers, editors, and research workers. Directed by Henry G. Alsberg, it employed sixty-six hundred men and women. The project's most important achievement was the American Guide series, which included guides for every state and territory (except Hawaii), as well as for the cities of Washington, D.C., New York, Los Angeles, San Francisco, New Orleans, and Philadelphia. It also produced guides for several major highways (U.S. 1, Ocean Highway, Oregon Trail), and for scores of towns, villages, and counties.

The detailed state guides combined travel information with essays on geography, architecture, history, and commerce. The project also produced ethnic studies, folklore collections, local histories, and nature studies, eventually producing a total of more than one thousand books and pamphlets.

The Federal Writers' Project funded such prominent authors of the 1930s as Conrad Aiken, Maxwell Bodenheim, Richard Wright, Ralph Ellison, Nelson Algren, Frank Yerby, Saul Bellow, and Weldon Kees, among many others. Congress ended federal sponsorship of the project in 1939 but allowed it to continue under state sponsorship until 1943.

Conclusion

President Roosevelt's wife Eleanor played an active role in promoting her husband's New Deal policy and programs. During her husband's presidency, she became an active lobbyist for civil rights legislation and joined the National Association for the Advancement of Colored People in 1939.

How Successful Was the New Deal?

Long after the 1929 stock market crash had stunned America, President Herbert Hoover was still clinging to the widely shared belief that American capitalism, with just a little help from the government (for industries, not individuals), would dispel the gathering depression. But the economy only continued its downward spiral.

Roosevelt promised—and delivered—"action and action now." His New Deal of "alphabet" agencies (AAA, NRA, WPA, SEC, FDIC, NLRB) and work-relief projects set the jobless to work building dams, bridges, highways, and airports. Congress enacted reforms that seemed radical to many at the time, such as Social Security, unemployment compensation, and federal insurance of bank deposits. By regulating banks and the stock market, the New Deal eliminated most of the dubious financial practices that had helped trigger the Great Depression.

Though there were those who hated him, by 1936 FDR had inspired enough public hope and confidence to win one of the most overwhelming electoral victories in U.S. history. To some, all this spelled revolution, though, except for the bloody battles fought by union organizers, strikers, and company goons at some factory gates, it was a remarkably peaceful one. FDR's New Deal philosophy did,

The National Industrial Recovery Act was enacted by the Congress of the United States to establish a new Public Works Administration (PWA) and to ensure orderly and fair competition by creating a National Recovery Administration (NRA) that drafted codes for industries.

after all, have something fundamentally in common with Hoover's beliefs: that Americans could take care of their own.

In each of its goals the New Deal was partially successful. The production controls and price supports managed by the National Recovery Administration and the Agricultural Adjustment Administration (both set up in 1933) helped put many business owners and farmers back on their feet, but the nation's economy did not regain its 1929 level until the United States entered World War II. The Public Works Administration (formed in 1933) and the Works Progress Administration (formed in 1935) helped tide many of the jobless over hard times, but nearly 9.5 million remained unemployed in 1939.

The Social Security Act of 1935 was another New Deal program criticized by some historians for those it failed to help—farmers, domestic help, and the elderly. However, from time to time since then, Congress amended this act to provide greater benefits, including the cost of living adjustment. At the time the Social Security Act was passed, its meager benefits were probably the only money some people saw for years. Roosevelt's New Deal also provided an early version of the food stamp program. The Social Security Act created a system of old-age pensions and unemployment insurance, and the Fair Labor Standards Act (1938) established a federal minimum wage and maximum-hours policy; both laws, however, excluded millions of working people.

After 1936 the New Deal was thrown increasingly on the defensive. The U.S. Supreme Court ruled that much of the New Deal legislation was unconstitutional, and the president's proposal in 1937 to enlarge the Court (to make it possible for him to appoint more liberal judges likely to be more receptive to New Deal legislation) caused many members of Congress to desert the president because they considered that proposal unconstitutional as well. In addition a severe recession (1937–1938) led many people to turn against New Deal policies.

When World War II erupted in September 1939, President Roosevelt grew increasingly reluctant to support reforms that might, by antagonizing conservatives in Congress or by alienating any bloc of voters, jeopardize support for his foreign policy. No major New Deal legislation was enacted after 1938.

Probably more than any of Roosevelt's social programs, it was the war that ultimately wrenched America free from the depression. Arms production stimulated industry. Before Roosevelt's second term was well under way, his domestic program was overshadowed by a new danger little noted by average Americans: the expansionist designs of totalitarian regimes in Japan, Italy, and Germany. In 1931 Japan invaded Manchuria and crushed Chinese resistance; a year later the Japanese set up the puppet state of Manchukuo. Italy, having succumbed to fascism, enlarged its boundaries in Libya and in 1935 attacked Ethiopia. Germany, where Adolf Hitler had organized the National Socialist Party and seized control of government in 1933, reoccupied the Rhineland and undertook large-scale rearmament.

At the end of the 1930s, the worldwide threat was no longer the depression but the rise to power of Adolf Hitler and the Nazi Party.

As the real nature of totalitarianism became clear, and as Germany, Italy, and Japan continued their aggression, many frightened Americans wanted to keep out of world affairs at all costs. In 1938, after Hitler had incorporated Austria into the German Reich, his demands for the Sudeten- land of Czechoslovakia made war in Europe seem possible at any moment. The United States, disillusioned by the

volved in the conflict look to it for aid. Neutrality legislation, enacted piecemeal from 1935 to 1937, prohibited trade with or credit to any of the warring nations. The objective was to prevent, at almost any cost, the involvement of the United States in a non-American war.

With the Nazi assault on Poland in 1939 and the outbreak of World War II, isolationist sentiment increased even more, even though Americans were far from neutral in their feelings about world events. Public sentiment clearly favored the victims of Hitler's aggression and supported the Allied powers that stood in opposition to German expansion. Under the circumstances, however, Roosevelt could only wait until public opinon regarding U.S. involvement was altered by events.

On September 1, 1939, Nazi Germany invaded Poland, precipitating the outbreak of World War II.

In a radio address in 1938, Roosevelt reminded the American people that

failure of the crusade for democracy in World War I, announced that in no circumstances could any country in-

democracy has disappeared in several other great nations, not because the people of those nations disliked democracy, but because they had grown tired of unemployment and insecurity, of seeing their children hungry while they sat helpless in the face of government confusion and government weakness through lack of leadership. Finally, in desperation, they chose to sacrifice liberty in the hope of getting something to eat. We in America know that our democratic institutions can be preserved and made to work. But in order to preserve them we need . . . to prove that the practical operation of democratic government is equal to the task of protecting the security of the people. The people of America are in agreement in defending their liberties at any cost, and the first line of the defense lies in the protection of economic security.[52]

Notes

Chapter One:
"Brother, Can You Spare a Dime?"

1. Quoted in Gail Stewart, *The New Deal*. New York: New Discovery Books, 1993, p. 45.
2. Quoted in Stewart, *The New Deal*, p. 44.
3. Quoted in David F. Burg, *The Great Depression: An Eyewitness History*. New York: Facts On File, 1996, p. 121.
4. Quoted in Burg, *The Great Depression*, p. 121.
5. "Roosevelt's First Inaugural Speech," *The History Channel*, http://www.historychannel.com/gsspeech/speeches/980914gs.htmc.
6. "Roosevelt's First Inaugural Speech," *The History Channel*, http://www.historychannel.com/gsspeech/speeches/980914gs.htmc.
7. Quoted in Burg, *The Great Depression*, p. 121.
8. "Roosevelt's Second Inaugural Speech," *The History Channel*, http://www.historychannel.com/gsspeech/speeches/980315gs.htmc.
9. Quoted in Studs Terkel, *Hard Times: An Oral History of the Great Depression*. New York: Pantheon, 1970, p. 31.
10. Quoted in Terkel, *Hard Times*, p. 20.
11. Quoted in Burg, *The Great Depression*, p. 101.
12. Quoted in Edward Robb Ellis, *A Nation in Torment: The Great American Depression 1929–1939*. New York: Coward-McCann, 1970, p. 230.
13. Quoted in Ellis, *A Nation in Torment*, pp. 229–230.
14. Quoted in Ellis, *A Nation in Torment*, p. 498.
15. Quoted in Lewis Lord, "The Rise of the Common Man," *U.S. News & World Report*, October 25, 1993, p. 10.
16. Quoted in Ellis, *A Nation in Torment*, p. 298.
17. Quoted in Burg, *The Great Depression*, p. 94.
18. Darlene Campbell, "Depression Cooking: How to Do It Without Getting Depressed!" *Countryside & Small Stock Journal*, vol. 78, no. 6, November/December 1994, p. 61.
19. Quoted in Ellis, *A Nation in Torment*, p. 237.
20. Quoted in Ellis, *A Nation in Torment*, p. 240.
21. Franklin D. Roosevelt, "Message to Congress, January 4, 1935," *New*

■

Deal Document Library, http:// newdeal.feri.org/speeches/1935a. htm.

22. "WPA Life Histories," Library of Congress, http://leweb2.loc.gov/.

23. Tillie Olsen, "The '30s," *Newsweek,* January 3, 1994, p. 24.

**Chapter Two:
Blowin' Down the Road**

24. Lawrence Svobida, *An Empire of Dust.* Caldwell, IN: Caxton Printers, 1940, p. 181.

25. "Farming the Dust Bowl," *PBS: The American Experience,* interview of Imogene Glover, www.pbs.org. wgbh/pages/amex/dustbowl/ eyewitness.html.

26. "Farming the Dust Bowl," interview of Judge Cowan.

27. "Farming the Dust Bowl," interview of Melt White.

28. Ann Marie Low, *Dust Bowl Diary.* Lincoln: University of Nebraska Press, 1984, p. 97.

29. University of South Dakota, *Grasshopper Plague,* www.webstersd. com/dirty30s/hopper/hoppers.htm.

30. "Farming the Dust Bowl," interview of J. R. Davidson.

31. Svobida, *An Empire of Dust,* p. 140.

32. Quoted in William Loren Katz, *An Album of the Great Depression.* New York: Franklin Watts, 1978, p. 37.

33. "Farming the Dust Bowl," inter-

view of Judge Cowan.

34. Quoted in Lord, "The Rise of the Common Man," p. 11.

35. Quoted in Lord, "The Rise of the Common Man," p. 11.

36. Quoted in Donald Worster, *Dust Bowl: The Southern Plains in the 1930s.* New York: Oxford University Press, 1979, p. 213.

37. Quoted in Worster, *Dust Bowl,* p. 213.

**Chapter Three:
Great Inroads for the
Labor Movement**

38. Quoted in Irving Bernstein, *Turbulent Years: A History of the American Worker, 1933–1941.* Boston: Houghton Mifflin, 1970, p. 2.

39. Franklin D. Roosevelt, "Message to Congress, June 8, 1934," www.ssa. gov.

40. Quoted in Terkel, *Hard Times,* p. 137

41. Quoted in Bruce Levine et al., *Who Built America?: Working People and the Nation's Economy, Politics, Culture, and Society.* New York: Pantheon, 1992, p. 385.

**Chapter Four:
In the News**

42. Quoted in Alan Jenkins, *The Thirties.* New York: Stein and Day, 1976, p. 169.

43. Quoted in Cabell Phillips, *From the Crash to the Blitz 1929–1939*. New York: Macmillan, 1969, p. 82.

Chapter Five:
The Golden Age of Radio

44. Quoted in Ellis, *A Nation in Torment*, p. 287.
45. Quoted in Donna Halper, History of Radio, http://www.oldtime.com/halper00.html.
46. Burns and Allen Homepage, http://members.tripod.com/bub25/burnsandallen2.html.
47. Charlie McCarthy Homepage, http://www.geocities.com/hollywood/academy/4534.
48. Radio Days: Private Eyes, http://www.otr.com/private.html.
49. Charlie Chan, http://www.cjnetworks.com/schmidtk/chan/chantalk.html.
50. "A Study in Scarlet," 221b Baker Street (Sherlock Holmes), http://www.sherylfranklin.com/sherlock.html.
51. Halper, History of Radio.

Conclusion:
How Successful Was
the New Deal?

52. "Economic Conditions" (recorded April 14, 1938), "FDR's Fireside Chats," from "Time and Again," *MSNBC On Air,* http://msnbc.com/Onair/msnbc/TimeAndAgain/archive/fdr/default.asp.

Chronology

1929

Herbert Hoover becomes president; stock market crash begins October 24; investors call October 29 "Black Tuesday."

1930

The first bank panic occurs; a public run on banks results in a wave of bankruptcies; John Wayne stars in his first western.

1931

No major legislation is passed addressing the depression; a second banking panic occurs in the spring; first of the Bonus Marchers descend on Washington, D.C.; Empire State Building is completed; singer Rudy Vallee has a hit with the song "Life Is Just a Bowl of Cherries."

1932

This and the next year are the worst years of the Great Depression; since 1930, industrial stocks have lost 80 percent of their value, 10,000 banks have failed since 1929, over 13 million Americans have lost their jobs since 1929, and farm prices have fallen 53 percent since 1929. Popular opinion considers Hoover's measures too little too late; Franklin Roosevelt easily defeats Hoover in the fall election and Democrats win control of Congress; newly elected Roosevelt pledges a New Deal for the American people. Al Capone is jailed for tax evasion; infant son of Charles Lindbergh is kidnapped and murdered; Jack Benny starts his radio career.

1933

Roosevelt inaugurated; begins "first 100 days" of intensive legislative activity; a third banking panic occurs in March; Roosevelt declares a bank holiday; closes financial institutions to stop a run on banks.

Congress authorizes creation of the Agricultural Adjustment Administration, the Civilian Conservation Corps, the Farm Credit Administration, the Federal Deposit Insurance Corporation, the Federal Emergency Relief Administration, the National Recovery Administration, the Public Works Administration, and the Tennessee Valley Authority.

Congress passes the Emergency Banking Bill, the Glass-Steagall Act of 1933, the Farm Credit Act, the National Industrial Recovery Act, and the Truth-in-Securities Act.

Frances Perkins is named secretary of

labor; Americans tune into FDR's first fireside chat; a jobless anarchist attempts to assassinate Roosevelt; first of the dust storms sweeps over the plains; prohibition is repealed; NY Giants defeat Washington Senators in World Series; first drive-in theater opens in Camden, NJ; popular songs include "Brother, Can You Spare a Dime?" and "It's Only a Paper Moon"; *King Kong* premiers in movie theaters.

1934

The economy turns around: GNP rises 7.7 percent, and unemployment falls to 21.7 percent; FBI ambushes and kills John Dillinger; Hitler rises to power in Germany; St. Louis Cardinals defeat Detroit Tigers in World Series; Bonnie and Clyde killed May 23 in Louisiana.

1935

The Supreme Court declares the National Recovery Administration to be unconstitutional; Congress authorizes creation of the Works Progress Administration, the National Labor Relations Board, and the Rural Electrification Administration.

Congress passes the Banking Act of 1935, the Emergency Relief Appropriation Act, the National Labor Relations Act, and the Social Security Act.

1936

FDR is reelected president; Jesse Owens wins four gold medals at the Berlin Olympics; Congress passes the Anti-Strikebreaker Act which declares it unlawful to transport or aid strikebreakers in interstate or foreign trade.

1937

General Motors recognizes the United Auto Workers union after their historic sit-down strike; first Social Security checks are sent out; pilot Amelia Earhart disappears over the Pacific; Joe Louis becomes heavyweight boxing champion.

1938

Congress passes the Agricultural Adjustment Act of 1938 and the Fair Labor Standards Act. (No major New Deal legislation is passed after this date, due to Roosevelt's weakened political power); FDR signs first minimum wage law (25 cents an hour); Swing Music fanatics mob Benny Goodman's band in New York.

1939

The depression is ending worldwide as economies gear up for the coming hostilities; World War II starts with Hitler's invasion of Poland; the "World of Tomorrow" world's fair opens in Flushing, NY.

For Further Reading

Maya Angelou, *I Know Why the Caged Bird Sings*. New York: Bantam Books, 1985. Award-winning African American author's autobiographical novel about growing up during the Great Depression.

William Loren Katz, *An Album of the Great Depression*. New York: Franklin Watts, 1978. Discusses the causes, events, and effects of the Great Depression and highlights the programs designed to alleviate it.

Edmund Lindop, *Modern America: The Turbulent Thirties*. New York: Franklin Watts, 1970. A survey of the political, economic, social, and cultural events and changes during the decade of the Great Depression.

Ann Marie Low, *Dust Bowl Diary*. Lincoln: University of Nebraska Press, 1984. Diary of a young woman who grew up in rural North Dakota during the depression.

Milton Meltzer, *Brother Can You Spare a Dime? The Great Depression*. New York: Facts On File, 1991. A history of the effects of the Great Depression on Americans in the 1930s, illustrated with contemporary photos.

Cabell Phillips, *From the Crash to the Blitz 1929–1939*. New York: Macmillan, 1969. A chronicle of American life during the Great Depression of the 1930s, based largely on material from the *New York Times*.

Upton Sinclair, *The Jungle*. New York: Penguin Books, 1965. A novel first published in the 1930s that described the terrible working conditions in Chicago's stockyards so vividly that FDR ordered an investigation of the meat-packing industry.

R. Conrad Stein, *The Great Depression*. Chicago: Childrens Press, 1993. Describes the 1929 stock market crash and the events and effects of the depression that followed, including the New Deal programs intended to restore the economy.

Gail Stewart, *The New Deal*. New York: New Discovery Books, 1993. Discusses the events leading up to America's Great Depression of the 1930s, Roosevelt's rescue of the event with the New Deal, and what caused the ultimate downfall of the New Deal.

Lawrence Svobida, *An Empire of Dust*. Caldwell, IN: Caxton Printers, 1940. The diary of a Kansas farmer recounting his dust bowl experiences.

Studs Terkel, *Hard Times: An Oral History of the Great Depression*. New York: Pantheon, 1970. A collection of interviews with Americans from different walks of life who lived through the Great Depression of the 1930s.

Women of Valor: The Struggle Against the Great Depression as Told by Their Own Life Stories. Chicago: J. R. Dee, 1990. A collection of biographies of American women who were influential during the 1930s in political, social, and labor reform.

Works Consulted

Books

Kenneth Allsop, *Hard Travelin': The Hobo and His History.* New York: New American Library, 1967. A history of how millions of unemployed men—and some women—hitched rides on flatcars, travelling throughout the United States in an often futile search for work.

Ralph K. Andrist, ed., *The American Heritage History of the 20's and 30's.* New York: American Heritage, 1970. U.S. history during the 1920s and 1930s, lavishly illustrated.

Anthony Badger, *The New Deal.* New York: Noonday Press, 1989. An in-depth study of FDR's programs to pull the United States out of the Great Depression during the 1930s.

Robert Bendiner, *Just Around the Corner: A Highly Selective History of the Thirties.* New York: Harper & Row, 1967. A study of radio, movies, and the arts during the Great Depression in the United States.

Irving Bernstein, *Turbulent Years: A History of the American Worker, 1933–1941.* Boston: Houghton Mifflin, 1970. A study of the American working class during the Great Depression.

Gary Dean Best, *The Nickel and Dime Decade: American Popular Culture During the 1930s.* Westport, CT: Praeger, 1993. A study of American movies, radio, games, sports, fads, and other diversions that helped people in the 1930s escape the poverty and anxiety of the Great Depression.

Ezra Bowen, ed., *This Fabulous Century,* vol. 4, *1930–1940.* Alexandria, VA: Time-Life Books, 1985. A coffee-table sized picture book depicting rural and city life in the United States during the 1930s.

David F. Burg, *The Great Depression: An Eyewitness History.* New York: Facts On File, 1996. An economic and social history of the 1930s; each chapter includes a section of quotations by famous political, artistic, and media figures appropriate to the topics being discussed.

Edward Robb Ellis, *A Nation in Torment: The Great American Depression 1929–1939.* New York: Coward-McCann, 1970. An in-depth study of the economic causes and effects of the Great Depression.

Lowell J. Endahl, "Electrification of Rural America," *Encyclopedia of*

Rural America. New York: Garland Publishing, 1990. History of the New Deal's efforts to bring electricity to rural America in the 1930s.

John Kenneth Galbraith, *The Great Crash: 1929.* Boston: Houghton Mifflin, 1972. A study of the causes and effects of the stock market crash of October 1929.

Otis L. Graham and Meghan Robinson Wander, *Franklin Roosevelt: His Life and Times.* New York: Da Capo Press, 1985. An encyclopedic treatment of FDR's politics, his personal life, and his New Deal programs.

Woody Guthrie, *Bound for Glory.* New York: E. P. Dutton, 1943. A compilation of Woody Guthrie's correspondence with other musicians during his lifetime, illustrated with sketches by the author.

D. S. Halacy Jr., *1936: The Picture Story of an Unforgettable Year.* New Rochelle, NY: Arlington House, 1963. A pictorial essay of the political, sports, and media highlights of 1936.

Laura Hapke, *Daughters of the Great Depression: Women, Work, and Fiction in the American 1930s.* Athens: University of Georgia Press, 1995. A study of women characters portrayed in literature set in the Great Depression.

Edwin P. Hoyt, *The Tempering Years.* New York: Charles Scribner's Sons, 1963. An in-depth study of the economic conditions that led to the Great Depression and of the New Deal programs that helped pull the United States back out.

R. Douglas Hurt, *Dust Bowl.* Chicago: Nelson-Hall, 1981. A study of rural life on the Great Plains during the depression years of the 1930s.

Alan Jenkins, *The Thirties.* New York: Stein and Day, 1976. A history of popular culture in the 1930s.

Arleen Keylin, ed., *The Depression Years, as Reported by the* New York Times. New York: Arno Press, 1976. A collection of headlines from the *New York Times* written during the 1930s, covering everything from politics and crime to music and sports.

Robert Lesser, *Pulp Art.* New York: Gramercy Books, 1997. Original cover paintings for the great American pulp magazines of the 1930s; includes biographical references.

Bruce Levine et al., *Who Built America?: Working People and the Nation's Economy, Politics, Culture, and Society.* New York: Pantheon, 1992. A report conducted by the City University of New York on its American Social History Project; part of the study is about working people in the 1930s.

Henry R. Luce, ed., *Time Capsule 1939.* New York: Time-Life Books,

1968. A history of the last year of the depression as the United States gears up to enter WWII, as condensed from the pages of *Time* magazine.

David Madden, ed., *Tough Guy Writers of the '30s*. Carbondale: Southern Illinois University Press, 1968. A study of writers such as Dashiel Hammett and their hard-boiled private eye characters.

Robert S. McElvaine, *The Great Depression: America 1929–1941*. New York: Random House, 1993. A history of the causes and effects of the Great Depression on American life from the Wall Street crash in 1929 to America's entry into WWII.

Deb Mulvey, ed., *We Had Everything but Money: Priceless Memories of the Great Depression*. New York: Crescent Books, 1995. Social life and customs of Americans during the depression.

Michael E. Parrish, *Anxious Decades: America in Prosperity and Depression 1920–1941*. New York: W. W. Norton, 1992. An overview of FDR's New Deal and the impact it had on America during the Great Depression.

Robert Peters, *Crunching Gravel: Growing Up in the Thirties*. San Francisco: Mercury House, 1988. A man remembers growing up in rural Wisconsin during the 1930s.

Albert U. Romasco, *The Poverty of Abundance: Hoover and the Great Depression*. New York: Oxford University Press, 1965. A study of American politics from the stock market crash of 1929 through the first year of Franklin Roosevelt's term in office, 1933.

Gene Smith, *The Shattered Dream: Herbert Hoover and the Great Depression*. New York: Morrow, 1970. A history of American politics from the stock market crash of 1929 through the first year of Franklin Roosevelt's term in office, 1933.

Robert Sobel, *The Great Bull Market: Wall Street in the 1920s*. New York: Norton, 1968. A history of the rise and fall of the New York Stock Exchange during the 1920s that helped cause the onset of the Great Depression of the 1930s.

Jerry Stanley, *Children of the Dust Bowl: The True Story of the Weed Patch Camp*. New York: Crown, 1992. Describes the plight of the migrant workers who traveled from the dust bowl to California during the depression and were forced to live in a federal labor camp, and discusses the school that was built for their children.

Harvey Swados, *The American Writer and the Great Depression*. Indianapolis:

Bobbs-Merrill, 1966. Part of the American Heritage series on twentieth-century writers.

Gordon Thomas, *The Day the Bubble Burst: A Social History of the Wall Street Crash of 1929.* Garden City, NY: Doubleday, 1979. Discusses the causes of the stock market crash and its effects on the U.S. economy through 1932.

Studs Terkel, *My American Century.* New York: New Press, 1997. A collection of interviews with people from different walks of life describing their experiences during the time period 1933–1945.

T. H. Watkins, *The Great Depression: America in the 1930s.* New York: Little, Brown & Company, 1993. The economic causes of the Great Depression and its effects on American society.

Susan Winslow, *Brother, Can You Spare a Dime? America from the Wall Street Crash to Pearl Harbor: An Illustrated Documentary.* New York: Paddington Press, 1976. A social and economic history of America from 1929 through the early 1940s.

Donald Worster, *Dust Bowl : The Southern Plains in the 1930s.* New York: Oxford University Press, 1979. Scientific and historical discussion of how the dust bowl affected Great Plains agriculture in the 1930s.

Periodicals

Darlene Campbell, "Depression Cooking: How to Do It Without Getting Depressed!" *Countryside & Small Stock Journal,* vol. 78, no. 6, November/December 1994. Offers information on cookery in country living, importance of creativity in feeding a family on a budget, usefulness of flour, value of sugar, preparation of potatoes, one-dish meals, and recipes from the depression era.

M. Golding, "Sweet Charity," *History Today,* vol. 41, no. 9, September 1991, p. 10. How Herbert Hoover tried in 1931 to recruit the heads of one hundred of the top businesses in the United States in an effort to have them start a private-sector fund-raising drive for charity.

David Goodman, "The Legacy of the CCC," *Ski Magazine,* vol. 59, no. 4, December 1994, p. 74. The story of the New Deal's Civilian Conservation Corps and how it helped transform the nation's parks.

Edward Holderby, "We Didn't 'Survive' the Depression: We Were Living!" *Countryside & Small Stock Journal,* vol. 79, no. 3, May/June 1995, p. 74. Living in rural America during the dust bowl of the 1930s.

Lewis Lord, "The Rise of the Common Man," *U.S. News & World Report,* October 25, 1993. A discussion of the American worker during the 1930s.

John A. Meyer, "Cigarette Century," *American Heritage,* vol. 43, no. 8, December 1992, p. 72. How the first evidence of the hazards of cigarette smoking appeared in the early 1930s when doctors began operating on their first cases of lung cancer.

Tillie Olsen, "The '30s," *Newsweek,* January 3, 1994. Novelist and essayist Olsen describes the ugliness and the beauty of the decade, the sense of country that emerged, images representing the decade that roused people to action, and what transformed the 1930s.

Bob Patton, "History of the Rural Electrification Industry," *Management Quarterly,* vol. 37, no. 4, Winter 1997, p. 7. History of the New Deal's efforts to bring electricity to rural America in the 1930s.

Peter Radetsky, "FDR and Polio Research," *World & I*, vol. 9, no. 4, April 1994, p. 388. The terrible polio epidemic during the 1930s and how FDR helped raise money for polio research.

Frances Seeber, "Eleanor Roosevelt and Women in the New Deal: A Network of Friends," *Presidential Studies Quarterly*, vol. 20, no. 4, Fall 1990, p. 707. A study of how influential Eleanor Roosevelt was in

New Deal policy and how she inspired American women to take a more active role in the social issues of the 1930s.

Roger Sharp, "Pinball!" *Popular Mechanics,* vol. 171, no. 12, December 1994, p. 63. A detailed history of how pinball was invented in the 1930s and why the game went on to become such a success.

Bradford Swift, "Keeping the Wolf from the Door," *Environmental Magazine*, vol. 5, no. 2, March/April 1994, p. 13. A history of how some of the New Deal's programs to help farmers during the dust bowl years still impact rural farmers today.

Websites

Burns and Allen Homepage, http://members.tripod.com/bub25/burnsandallen2.html. A history of the career of this comedy couple from their vaudeville days, through radio and into TV and movies, with soundbites.

Charlie Chan, http://www.cjnetworks.com/schmidtk/chan/chantalk.html. An overview of the detective character Charlie Chan from the radio dramas of the 1930s to film adaptations of the '40s and '50s, with soundbites and video clips.

Charlie McCarthy Homepage, http://www.geocities.com/hollywood/

academy/4534. A history of the program with pictures of the characters and soundbites from some of the more famous episodes.

"Farming the Dust Bowl," *PBS: The American Experience,* www.pbs.org. wgbh/pages/amex/dustbowl/ eyewitness.html. An overview of the PBS television documentary, with soundbite excerpts of the interviews with dust bowl survivors.

Donna Halper, History of Radio, http://www.oldtime.com/halper00. html. A series of four essays written in 1997 by a broadcast historian from Emerson College discussing the development of radio programs during the 1930s, with music and program soundbites.

Radio Days: Private Eyes, http:// www.otr.com/private.html. An overview of the various private eye dramas that became popular in the 1930s and 1940s, with soundbites.

Franklin D. Roosevelt, "Message to Congress, June 8, 1934," www.ssa.gov. This site is sponsored by the U.S. government and features a collection of important presidential speeches.

Franklin D. Roosevelt, "Message to Congress, January 4, 1935," *New Deal Document Library,* http://newdeal.feri. org/speeches/1935a.htm.

"Roosevelt's Second Inaugural Speech," *The History Channel,* http://www. historychannel.com/gsspeech/ speeches/980315gs.htmc. Part of the History Channel's on-line collection of FDR's most famous speeches.

"A Study in Scarlet," 221b Baker Street (Sherlock Holmes),http:// www.sherylfranklin.com/sherlock. html. An overview of all the Sherlock Holmes radio episodes, with soundbites.

University of South Dakota, *Grasshopper Plague,* www.webstersd.com/ dirty30s/hopper/hoppers.htm. Study of the effects of grasshopper infestations in South Dakota during the depression; includes interviews of farmers who lived through it.

"WPA Life Histories," Library of Congress, http://leweb2.loc.gov/. The Library of Congress has catalogued a number of the life histories WPA writers were commissioned to write in the 1930s as part of the New Deal, and has made them available through their site on the Internet.

Index

Picture Credits

About the Author

Petra Press writes non-fiction for children and young adults, video scripts, and TV documentaries. Some of her most recent projects include books on settling the United States, Native American peoples, recent immigrants to the United States, and AIDS.